The Girl Who Would Not Stay Down

The Girl Who Would Not Stay Down

Annie Scott

autho**rHOUSE®**

AuthorHouse™ UK Ltd.
1663 Liberty Drive
Bloomington, IN 47403 USA
www.authorhouse.co.uk
Phone: 0800.197.4150

Published by AuthorHouse   10/21/2013

ISBN: 978-1-4918-8156-9 (sc)
ISBN: 978-1-4918-8157-6 (e)

Dedication

I would like to dedicate this book
to my darling daughter Nicola.
She has encouraged me, reminded me of things,
assisted me in every way and been a great help.
Sons are great but daughters are FABULOUS.
Thanks Nikki.

Foreword

"Having grown up in a very unconventional family, this book opened my eyes to many of the reasons as to why I am the person I have become today.

When I asked my mother Annie Scott to write her life story I had no idea of the ride we were in for. Today I contentedly reside in a sleepy little town in Australia, which is my safe haven and I am thankful for it.

I am thrilled to be able to assist my mother in telling the world how three generations of women carved their way through life's extraordinary struggles. And in passing their history on to the next two generations will keep their stories alive. I hope their journey inspires you too."
N. Scott (daughter of Annie)

Preface and Acknowledgement

The aim of this autobiography is to inform my family of the reasons for the many personality quirks of their mother. Life is like a colouring book, the basic outlines are there but circumstances dictate the colours and my circumstances were vivid . . . I began life as an innocent, unsuspecting little girl to be thrust into a palette of shocking hues shown to me by eccentric characters who were my family. I have been coloured by life to a large extent but feel quite proud to have remained fairly sane—I think. Judge for yourself and enjoy a good read.

Introduction

After marrying a cruel bully, I escaped with my children and had many adventures. Eventually I fell for a second love who I thought would be our saviour, only to take my family out of the frying pan into the fire. He was to be the most dangerous of all and only extreme good luck and quick thinking saved us from certain death.

Enjoy this account of life through the decades and be sure to take warning of what can happen to an innocent who is unprepared for **what lies ahead.**

Chapter One

I was a very determined child, living in a pretty town in a farming community where the main crops were apples, pears and plums. They were mainly 'growers' in Worcestershire. Orchards abounded and red brick houses were most often seen. Our house was large and sited detached on a common in Malvern. Our front view was the Malvern Hills, stately and picturesque.

Although a picture postcard town and attracting many tourists now, in those days it was quiet and simple with a very narrow attitude. It was first settled long, long ago, more than 1000 years B.C. and it is a lovely destination for those who love walking, archaeology and bracing air. The British Camp, a part of the Malvern Hills, has got all three.

In the 1940's when I was born, it was parochial and required a fresh influx of blood, which fortunately it was to get. However, it had *had* its grand times, the waters brought many Victorians to drink them and have freezing cold immersions and wrappings in cold watery sheets.

In those times, sufferers of aches and pains thought that the cold, pure water would help cure them. Consequently there are some lovely old hotels in the town and it is fun imagining the coaches drawing up outside them and the ostlers (*grooms*), busying about the horses. The wealthy occupants preparing to be frozen all in the name of a cure for rheumatics. Eventually people realised it was best to just *drink* the stuff.

There are many fern clad Springs, tinkling into small wells at the base of the hills, these are 'dressed' nowadays and competitions are held for which is the most beautifully or originally done. They contain crystal clear cold water so beloved by the past visitors. Nowadays, the royal household uses Malvern water, for drinking. It is incredibly pure. There is a main well called St Ann's. This one is actually on the hill and a path leads from it to the Beacon, the highest hill, with a view over fifteen counties from the top. The well was named after Christ's grandmother, she was called Ann. I am now a grandmother and I find that awfully touching, I never thought of Christ having a grandma before—it is also said to have a Ley line passing through it. Yes, Malvern has its mystical side.

It was a little climb up the hill to the well and a long steep one to the Beacon, but in the old days, there were donkeys with side saddles for the ladies who wished to ride. Poor donkeys, but Mrs. Bettridge, who owned them, made a small fortune so I expect she treated them well. Queen Victoria went up there, and there is a photo of her on a donkey sitting side saddle, ladies didn't ever ride astride in those days. As well as visiting St Ann's well, she actually rode right up to the top of the Beacon. The highest hill of the range was named long ago. In case of possible invasion, a lit bonfire up there would show far and wide. Thank heavens the Spanish didn't come—people lived in fear of it throughout the land. Fancy wanting to invade when our weather isn't a patch on theirs, we very sensibly 'invade' them now.

Would you believe, I actually ended up with one of the very same side saddles. It was given to me when I was young and horsey, by a very old lady who was living in a huge granite stone house in Malvern. She was a member of an old family of Confectioners. Two of the great names in those times were Cadbury and Caley. Caley's was based in Norwich and still is, it started business in the eighteen hundreds and chocolates were sent to the front in the first world war by the company. Miss Caley, a relative, lived alone in Malvern. I suppose being wealthy, it would have been a beautiful part of the country to choose to make home. She kept a cute but stubborn bay pony in her house. *Yes, I do mean in her house.* As friends of hers also knew me, I was called upon to visit and ride him. There he was, amongst the straw happily munching away in the parlour. His name was Joey and she wanted me to ride him with the local hunt, as he was eating his droppings and losing condition. She thought exercise would do the trick. He was too stubborn though and not able to be handled by one as young as me. I was forced to accept defeat and the rather eccentric Miss Caley and I parted company sadly, me clutching the side saddle that she had received from Mrs Bettridge years ago and obviously no longer used. I admired it and she gave it to me as a present. It had no worm in the *tree* (that is the wooden frame that the leather is built up on). It was a real beauty and so old. It was a miracle that it was in such lovely condition after all those years.

I wonder what became of Joey? He needed a vet and keeping in a field really—but he was her companion.

Years later, I let the lovely saddle go to a London antique dealer to pay school fees, which were keeping me poor. It is a shame though, it had such a history and it could have seated Queen Victoria.

In Malvern there are many private schools, the most spectacular though, is undoubtedly Malvern College. Malvern College boards both boys and girls and I understand, has become co-educational now. When I was a child, the sexes were in two separate colleges. They are impressive buildings built from granite obtained from quarries in the hills. The quarrying has long since stopped, but when I was a girl, I regularly heard great explosions when they were at work.

The granite was tough and superb. It often gleamed with a pinkish hue. In the Silurian age, 400 million years ago, waves lapped at shores which, when the tectonic plates shifted, allowed the sea water to drain below the crust. This caused an upheaval which made the land rise. The ensuing 'folds' were pushed up to become Malvern's hill range, causing the hilly ridge, which accounts for the little sea shells I used to find on them. That section was under the sea once, amazing. How our world came about is stupendous to think of, it staggers me . . . I have tried to explain how the hills happened, I think it is right, but I do not know all the technical terms for the geology involved in the creation of them. I just remember puzzling over the sea shells lying around when I was young and riding my pony up there.

A past friend of mine from my younger days had a house with an external kitchen wall left natural and unplastered. It was made entirely of beautiful Malvern granite, which glistened and had ferns growing out of it—I guess in retrospect that he had probably planted them in the little folds and crevices. The trouble was it got very damp when it rained. With the spot lights shining on it, it was spectacular. His house was on the side of the hill and going out of the back door was a bit of a climb if you were not young. I often wondered how long it would be for anyone living there, before arthritis set in. The back garden was the hills, covered in foxgloves—so natural and colourful with many Rowan trees which looked spectacular in autumn. Lots of wild and lovely creatures visited, especially red deer. To my young mind, it would have been the perfect place to live, who cared about the drawbacks when one was just a girl.

The schools had a special tunnel at the railway station, for the young pupils to walk to their carriages. They would then deliver the doting Mammas and children to their respective colleges. It was all very genteel and convenient, *if you were the very well off.* I would think that life was rather wonderful, to be there in such a beautiful setting.

Chapter Two

In the past, my Grandmother discovered Malvern when she and her husband (a Surgeon) had stayed there. He had originally spent a lot of time in London working at Great Ormond Street Hospital. He had also been the junior partner in a practice of physicians who looked after the Royal family.

At that time he was married to Catharine Amy Dawson—Scott, she founded the P.E.N. writers club which was to become a 'mighty' organisation. She was a real 'blue stocking' totally brilliant and unconventional. Her world was writers, poets, artists and intellectualism. I think it was all too much for him, his love was medicine and he became disinterested with his wife's causes, no matter how worthy and his home was always filled with young aspiring writers and poets who Catharine was feeding and encouraging.

He met my Grandmother whilst treating her and the rest as we say, is history.

The doctor and Grandmother took their daughter out on special days from school, in a Landau, a carriage pulled by horses. After he died, because her original family came from the area and she thought the town so beautiful, she moved her family to Malvern from Wales and bought the villa, where they settled.

For a little income as well as an interest, she taught Ballroom dancing, as she was a good dancer and a good

6

and patient teacher. They used to dance in the front room which had a lovely floor and was spacious. The family had a life as full as possible with loads of friends. Her personality drew people to her and she was vivacious.

Being independent and no longer so sad and having recovered with the help of time after his death, she decided to buy a Chevrolet car and was the first lady driver in Worcestershire. Although she did tell me that she rolled backwards and ran over a policeman's toe on Porlock Hill once. Well it was a one in four gradient and driving in Somerset, in those days, it was hard to avoid. That hill on the A 39 has to be driven with care because of the hairpin bends. There is now a road that avoids the hill, if a driver wishes an alternative.

Grandma wouldn't have taken a driving test, simply because, they didn't exist in those days. The policeman let her off though as she was very attractive with blue eyes and long wavy black hair which she kept in a chignon at the back of her neck. She was quite petite and had blocks on the pedals in the car to be able to reach them. To be good looking was, and is and always will be, very handy. Despite the freedom of being a wealthy widow, she did miss her older partner Horatio though. He looked after her and gave her status.

As a child, she had been the daughter of a gentleman farmer. I remember her telling me that she used to wear a 'poke bonnet' as a little girl and swing on five-barred gates whilst waiting to open them for farmers taking their animals and geese to market. If she was lucky, they would throw her a penny.

In the eighteen eighties, there no way of transporting stock to market other than walking it there. If the farm was a long way from the town, they had no option. Therefore, farmers 'drove' their sheep, cows and geese along country lanes and often at night the farmer slept at an Inn, (if there was one near) and the farm boys were obliged to sleep alongside the stock. Grandma said that they had a terrible time getting the livestock ready to continue the next morning, as the geese would have all roosted in the nearest trees to avoid foxes. Getting them down and grouped together for walking onwards to the town, must have been a nightmare. Life was so tricky without a nice lorry to load up . . . it looks quaint on paintings, but as with much of life in those times, it was no picnic.

Imagine having to draw water from the pump on washing day . . . the weight of carrying the buckets into the house and the icy water in winter time. Even getting it dry must have been shocking with no tumble driers in the winter. When plumbing arrived and the water was piped indoors, it must have been heaven for the women. Before boilers were developed, warming it on the old ranges must have taken ages. It was no wonder that all their life was taken up with struggling to exist and they died young compared with modern times. Only the Aristocracy could have had time to play, handing over the drudgery to others. Everyone else was just coping from day to day. Old folk had to be maintained in the family group, they wouldn't have had the strength to chop the wood to heat the ranges. They mostly would have been used to mind the babies, whilst the more able young, did the heavy stuff.

Although progress is inevitable, with the coming of technology, it is perfectly possible to bypass the really old people; their use has ceased to exist now. I see these poor old folks when I go to the shops, sitting looking sad and alone, watching the world hurry past them.

The fit and able seniors, often still have the children, the Mothers just go to work. I remember my mother being shocked at this, the elderly grandparents however, like to be useful and *'the bank of Mum and Dad'* is becoming more essential for home deposits and educational trips for their children's kids. I expect that my mother having to work solidly all her life felt that retiring should mean doing as little work as possible.

Chapter Three

To continue with the story . . . My maternal Great Grandfather's family produced several sons who were Grandma's uncles. One, flew planes being an aerial photographer in the 1914-'18 war and subsequently was killed. Another became a very fine musician. He became a famous cathedral organist and also later, played on early radio. Another farmed in Malvern and his family is there to this day, he has several sons too. My Great Grandfather became a successful farmer and fruit grower, he resided outside Malvern.

His daughter, my Grandma, was the problem child however. She was wilful and a terrible trial to her gentle mother who was dying of breast cancer. She got in terrible rages for the least little thing and had a fierce temper. Despite all, when her mother passed away, she must have missed her terribly at such a tender age. Her father Charles, my Great Grandfather, must have been so lonely—but he did eventually marry again.

Grandma told me that she saw her mother after she had passed away. There was a style at the bottom of the garden. It separated the garden from the honeysuckled lane, which bordered it. Her Mother stood at the other side of the style. Grandma being a very little girl when her mother died did not remember in detail how she looked. She *was* however, said to describe the lady so exactly, that everyone was shocked to realise that it could only have been her. Then she said, the lady asked her a question . . . *"Are you being a good girl Lizzie"?* As she related this to the open mouthed, father and brothers, it was quite a sensation and was to be discussed for years.

Grandma was soon to go down with a serious attack of measles, maybe she hallucinated? She may have had a very high temperature? Who knows . . . It would be foolish not to keep an open mind to the spiritual. One doesn't have to be religious to do that. I will tell of other weird things of a spiritual nature, later in my account.

Her father, remarried again. It was to the cook. A woman called Annie. Grandma didn't get on with Annie the Cook. She handed out some much needed discipline to the young Lizzie. I think she was allowed to give her some 'thrashings' (*according to Grandmother's account*). Maybe that is why my Grandma, beat her own daughter so relentlessly, they say it perpetuates.

Great Grandfather was a bit of a character; he climbed an apple tree to prune it at the age of 65, fell out and broke his hip. He recovered, but had a limp after that. It is a wonder he did so well in those days but he lived to 96 years and was much loved by us all. Including his daughter Lizzie . . . even though she told me that he used to *wallop* her regularly with a stick.

For a while all was fine. Grandmother and her four children were socially up with the best families. She was the toast of the little community with her dancing, good looking youngsters and motor car. In life, disaster is never far away however and it certainly came to them.

The first change in her fortunes came when the stocks and shares which *she should have sold when she could,* became worth nothing. The Irish railways were taken over by the state and nationalised. She really should have obtained a good Broker to mind her business interests.

Her first husband who was not kind to her, died in an industrial accident. Her second love, the doctor had been half Irish and half Scottish. He was born in Northern Ireland in a large white house in Portadown. He drank a little, brandy mainly, but he wasn't a slave to it like Grandma's first husband. Grandma's first husband had been a serious drinker and abused her. Undoubtedly, that was how she met the next love, whilst being patched up after sustaining some blows from the first. They didn't intend it but they fell in love. He was considerably older than she was and nicknamed her 'kiddie'. No doubt he was shocked and disgusted at her first husband's mistreatment and she would have felt safe and somewhat infatuated with him. Nothing grows love faster than kindness and she needed that after her unhappy marriage. She must have been hard to resist with her looks and personality. She was well read too and a good conversationalist. He must have been dazzled with her obvious interest in him and thoroughly flattered.

He was an aristocrat with a *coat of arms* from a very old family that went to the crusades. He was wealthy. He was also married. He was so dazzled and enchanted that he left his first family. It caused terrible repercussions although Catharine his wife never stopped loving him. He loved his children very much and it must have been dreadful for him to be without them. Catharine was a prolific writer and produced many books; she was also a great socialite, a friend of Noel Coward and other great authors and notables. She would have had her writing and her founding of the P.E.N. Writers club to help her over the pain—but he must have wept many tears over the loss of his children.

He was handling life until he met Grandmother and then he lost his head, as so many men do over a pretty younger woman. Previously he had, before working at Great Ormond street hospital, been travelling the world as the ship's doctor on a yacht. Yachts looked very different in those days. They tended to be painted black, not white, and had dark sails. It was a sturdy craft however, and his travels took him all over the world.

His big love was Norway. The amazing glaciers and the ancient Norse religion with their 'Gods and folklore' fascinated him. He took stunning photographs of the scenery as it was before the planet started warming up. Photography was his hobby and it passed on to my mother, she processed all her pictures which was rather rare for a woman, in those days.

When he travelled with the yacht, to the West Indies and other distant lands, he took many fascinating photographs that I still have. This was early photography in sepia. The photo's have not kept all that well, they are very old. They are interesting though and one is of his yacht and there is a West Indian woman loaded up with yams and other goodies for sale in a dish on her head. I will try to include one or two in this book.

When his travels took him to the West Indies he went for interesting characters to shoot rather than the scenery. He also found Colombia fascinating in those days; I bet it still is I would love to go there. He spent time in Cartagena and took many photographs. Although I have never been there, I adored that 1984 film 'Romancing the Stone' with Michael Douglas and Kathleen Turner which purports to be Colombian scenery—it was actually shot in Mexico but the terrain must be similar to the mountains and jungle scenes that are so thrilling in the film. Although 1984 is a long time ago, that movie is still fabulous and the scenery great. *It always gives me itchy feet.* Maybe one day . . .

The ports (which he constantly used—being on a yacht) looked very simple; they were just corrugated tin sheds. There are various streets photographed with the indigenous population carrying baskets on their heads and markets with many donkeys heaving fruit and vegetables in their carts. There were no cars of course, just the donkeys with their loads of bananas, bread fruit and the usual items of sale in that area. The fruits would have been unknown back here at home at that time, apart from perhaps by the few adventurous souls who travelled, or what was grown in the greenhouses of the fashionable, *mainly pineapples as producing those was a great status symbol.*

Even so, in those days they would probably have done the Italian Tour which was fashionable. Only the few went as far as Africa, the West Indies or The Americas.

He sent his children post cards of exotic places. They spent their summers in Cornwall. I wonder if he was deliberately putting distance between his wife and himself. Maybe he was ready to wander to another woman?

Divorce was rare in those days, a Gentleman always allowed his wife to divorce him, whether he was the guilty party or not. He *was* of course. My Mother had already been conceived.

Later when mother was an older girl, there was much to be told, but for the moment I will jump ahead to when she was grown to womanhood.

Chapter Four

Mother was not an easy person to know, petite and attractive, she was alas argumentative and had a shocking temper. She also had Aspergers and coupled with a degree of Paranoia, growing up with her made life super hard sometimes for me—but I loved her.

She was very *noticeable*, with pale skin and dark hair, probably the Gaelic complexion as her father was the product of an Irish Mother and Scottish father. Her figure was perfect as she probably didn't ever have too much food or too much rest, her circumstances being what they were. Her difficult temper was doubtless inherited from her mother. I received lots of discipline as a child, mainly for "back-chatting" as she called it. She was always saying that she would knock me into the middle of next week. I think that meant—put me into a coma. That generation believed in no nonsense, but I doubt they ever analyzed what their threats actually meant. When I was eighteen she slapped me for the last time, I suggested that she didn't do that again otherwise there might be repercussions, and she got the message.

My Mother really liked best to hide away, as getting on with people was difficult. She didn't make friends socially and preferred not to go out to dinner or parties, as she was misunderstood when she voiced her forthright opinions, and subsequently ended up feeling mortified. She was terribly sensitive and people just didn't see things her way, as her words would come out wrongly. This caused her to dislike people in general. She particularly seemed to loath men.

Her first marriage failed, just as her Mother's had. She could see only one point of view which didn't help. Grandmother's was for the reason of abuse by her first husband but that certainly wasn't to be mother's reason.

I grew up confused, being a reasonably attractive teenager, I attracted the opposite sex—I found myself excusing them all the time. Mum would condemn them; I would speak up in their defence. She would say they only had one thing on their mind. Probably true, but at fifteen, cynical thought has not had time to occur. It was hard to form my own opinions about the world, boys, the reasons for living, without her banging away with her prejudiced viewpoint.

However, my natural optimistic turn of mind (which was to stand me in good stead later in my life) kept me full of the joys of youth.

It was a good thing that Mother went to her laboratory to work. Being clever, she helped with miniaturisation of component parts that went in rockets. She grew crystals and made tiny component parts which I assume the crystals went in but I didn't know what went on as she was not expected to tell too much to the general public. Britain had a space program of its own then—'Blue Streak' was the project. She had an opposite number in America and helped work with him. I remember her mentioning 'Black Night' too, I can't imagine what that was but everything was eventually discontinued due to finance I suppose. I wish that I had taken more interest in her side of things, but I had a young person's busy outlook and a million things to do concerning my newly married life in London.

Eventually, the whole thing was taken over by the USA because they were in the space race and in those days, money was no object over there, where as we had just come through a very expensive time, the War. Her work must have assisted though and in that respect she was very happy—she adored her job.

As a child she was a very clever girl, winning the 'Victor Ludorum'. It was the award for coming top in every subject, at her Girls school. She was especially good at physics.

She also took piano lessons and became exceptional. I am sure that she would have gained a scholarship to further her talent. Her mother would not have dreamed of letting her go on to a conservatoire to study and make music her living. Instead, she took her away from school and sent her to work. It was tragic in her case.

Grandma needed her to make money *sooner* rather than later. It was sad putting money before one's child's career. If only her father had been alive. She was to grow up always feeling cheated, but girls were considered less important in those days.

Education was geared to the male. Girls were expected to marry and have babies and become the property of the husband. There must have been many girls, unable to follow the profession they wanted, with conventional parents not willing to pay for their education beyond a certain level. The life of Beatrix Potter is a prime example. Her Mother positively discouraged her to do anything. She showed great determination becoming a writer. It took the Second World War to make the necessary changes in women's fortunes.

Mum's mother, my grandmother, being a farmer's daughter, probably would have been the reason for our great love of horses.

Grandma had photographs of her sons, my uncles, jumping *triple gates* leading a horse either side, a fete of amazing daring—competing for their horse regiments in gymkhanas, before they became mechanised.

Chapter Five

Grandmother's husband had really gone through it, what with all that followed after the First World War when he had really suffered. He ceased working at Great Ormond St. Hospital; it doesn't take much working out that a scandal must have followed as he was such an important doctor. He moved to a quiet practise in Cwmaman, in Aberdare. It was a mining valley, where he looked for peace after what he had been through. In the war, he had had to administer the *'coup de grace'* in an execution . . . He, being the medical officer in charge and the poor soldier being accused of cowardice. He was so shattered that he nearly lost his mind. Trouble seemed to follow him though, as there was a pit disaster and he had to carry out an amputation of a man trapped by his leg underground.

The Doctor, poor man, was suffering from depression and I suspect, struggling with Aspergers . . . although it wasn't known about in those days. Having had survived a marriage break-up, losing his beloved children from his first wife, not to mention his reputation and also living with Grandmother, who was rather 'flighty'. *She sold kisses at a charity ball and mortified him.* Such things were not 'done' in his class, but Grandma thought it a good idea and it raised an awful lot of money. So, all in all, his life wasn't a bed of roses.

She was also understandably intolerant regarding alcohol, and doubtless, nagged him. Eventually, he found the answer in his depressed mind. After a sad and uncomfortable few years, he took his own life by poison—a terrible way to die. Poisons were easily obtained at Aberdare's big hospital where he worked. He obviously needed to suffer. Perhaps he thought it would bring atonement. He was missing for a long time before he was found dead, behind the hospitals fixed back, big front doors. Grandma was in shock and retired to her bed, not to get up for a very long time, a classic symptom of depression. Life for Grandma's four children changed dramatically then, out of their schools they came and into the world of earning their own money.

Mother smocked *shantung* silk dresses for a rich child and helped look after her. The parents used to talk French in front of mother, not realising that she spoke it better than they did. Sadly, all traces of privilege ended sharply, when her mother married again. This time it was to her gardener.

This caused a huge scandal in Malvern. The snobby friends thought that she had married beneath her and crossed her off their visiting list. I doubt if this unduly worried her though, as he was very handsome and half her age—he was twenty two and she was forty two. Mother disliked him as she had heard the obvious talk, Malvern being a hotbed of gossip.

The young husband had a day job at the local Tennis Park. He gardened for Grandma at weekends.

He was a very accomplished 'Grounds man', making and maintaining the wonderful grass and hard courts that many *'greats'* used to play on before continuing to Wimbledon. Fred Perry and Dan Maskell knew him well. My Step Grandfather *'hobnobbing' with* famous Sportsmen and women must have had many tales to tell at home.

He must have been interesting company and in fact, was offered a job at Wimbledon. Grandma talked him out of that though. She would not have been 'Queen Bee' in that area and would not have *'wiped the eye'* of her detractors for marrying a guy half her age. So they stayed put in Malvern. However, they were to remain married for all of my Grandmother's life.

The young husband also had a great sense of humour, he was always committing pranks and I adored him as a little one. I was a toddler, but can remember a lady coming to our house and my step Grandfather asking her to look through a little brass kaleidoscope. Needless to say, the end of it was well rubbed in soot and she had a perfect ring around her eye. She seemed to take it very well. In those days, things were simpler. I can't imagine what she would have said or done now. That is one of my first memories. It is so *lovely that it was such a happy one.*

It was no wonder that Grandma's head was turned, but the marriage did cause a great deal of scandal.

His father drank, was it surprising? No, the poor man had lost a son in the Arctic Convoys; the young fellow had to be prised away from the gun on the ship, his fingers frozen to it. He was one of the many who bravely risked both appalling seas and weather, taking supplies to the starving Russians. Alas, he was killed by the Germans although, just a boy. It is only now in 2013 that 'Arctic Star' medals are being supplied to the few men remaining. Those still alive are extremely old men. Posthumous 'Arctic Star' medals are also being struck and the families will be receiving them at last. My step Grandfather's brother was a hero, but it is terribly hard to live with loss and that is why in my opinion, there was alcoholism in his family.

Grandma being teetotal said that Jack would have to become teetotal if they were going to live together and be happy. He obviously saw a loving woman, a moneyed lifestyle and a better way of life. It was an easy decision to make, there was never to be drink in the house from that day onwards, but he had a comfortable existence thence forth. A lifetime later, when Grandma had died and he was left to do as he wanted, he went back to alcohol in a big way. It shows one thing, for love it is possible to radically change your habits. Anyway, they were married and were happy together.

Years later I remember, when V.J. day came (Victory over Japan) and I was in my little flag dress, being very small, Grandma's young husband Jack, dressed in drag and with dark glasses, wandered about shaking hands and no one knew who he was. He made a wonderful little old lady wearing black.

It was a great celebration, tables in the road, everyone dressed in fancy dress and there were scrumptious goodies to eat. After war time privations, our young eyes were glued to the food. I was fortunate to never have to go short as grandma kept chickens and ducks. Many items of food were never seen though, in those days. Seeing tables of cakes was a huge novelty. I was too young to remember the first victory celebrations. I bet they were something.

Mother's dislike of Grandma's third husband went down like a lead balloon. It caused her to be treated cruelly for her opinions and beaten. As a young teenager, doubtless she wasn't the easiest girl to live with. Teenagers generally aren't and she had been through trauma. Nothing excused the thrashings she received though, with a cane. Grandmother was beaten as a girl and perhaps the cycle continues, they say it does. I certainly didn't beat my kids though.

She had a very bitter and cruel mother who had a mean streak and took it out on the youngest daughter. She really only loved her boys. Mother had to slave for them too and iron their shirts, how she loathed that. She was the only child by the doctor and doubtless the most difficult.

Her older sister and brothers belonged to Grandma's first husband. He was later killed in an industrial accident, conveniently freeing Grandma. No wonder Mother was strange and difficult for me to live with as I grew older. She had *had* such an unkind mother. Her childhood was also very sad because she had one lifestyle and was plunged into an entirely different one. From having servants, *she* became the servant and all at the tender age of fourteen.

During Mother's dressmaking days, she also had a weekend job to earn her keep at home. Grandmother didn't see Motherhood as modern parents do. She relieved Mother of most of her earnings even though she was so young. Nowadays, the young see staying at home as a chance to help save a deposit for their first home, for college debt or that foreign holiday. Plenty do not even give money over to their parents for keep. Believe me, life was so different between the wars, it was hard. She worked on days off, at Malvern Boys College in the Tuck shop.

There she met and became infatuated with an older man, a House Master. He was twice her age. She doubtless saw a 'father figure' and was craving affection and attention. He, being charmed by her intelligence and petite figure, was attracted to her. Meeting her illicitly, he seduced her and she became pregnant. This was a fearful scandal in those days, and she was only a youngster herself, a teenager.

Chapter Six

The House Master was a well regarded man married to a vicar's daughter. Modern times would see him as a Paedophile. He specialised in impregnating young girls and had several illegitimate children all over Malvern.

The times and his wealth and the fact that he was from an old moneyed aristocratic family, protected him. He had free rein and must have caused havoc in such a small town. Maybe he thought of himself as a Squire of old, sampling the local maidens. He must have thought that he had the 'The Right of the Lord of the Manor.' The local Lord would have first dibs at the young virgins. I suppose to make sure that his genes were spread around in the days of inter-breeding. It must have been awful and it wasn't too good for Mother, even if she brought it on herself. He was old enough to know better, they weren't feudal times. However, my devastated Mother was sent to a private nursing home in South London and paid for by him to have her child, my sister and given her name by him.

My sister was named 'Daphne' a name which for some reason she loathed for life. I think it is a lovely old fashioned name but I expect she wanted to be thoroughly modern, a Gillian or June.

The nursing home was not too far from the old Crystal Palace. As Mother was being driven to it, being in labour with my sister, she saw the Crystal Palace burning down. It was an amazing sight with melted glass running in the gutters.

I have often wondered if she really did see this incredible sight first hand, she was taking cancer drugs when she told me this, I think she had dreamed about it so often that she believed the fact to be true. My sister's birth year in relation to mine doesn't match up if she really saw it, but I love the story. Some said that it had been losing money for quite a while, and was probably an *insurance job*—I wonder if that was true? I personally doubt it, fires can easily occur in old buildings with rubbish lying about, a person would have only to have dropped a cigarette. It was not paying its way by then. I would have loved to have seen it myself though. I and my children only saw the original stone statues of prehistoric monsters that were at the base of the steps. They used to play there sometimes, in the Crystal Palace Park, when we lived in South London. It must have been a wonderful place with the sun gleaming on it, at the top of the hill. It even had its own railway station then. Parts of that are still there and are rumoured to have a ghost.

Regarding my mother's pregnancy, it was true that life had radically altered by then for young girls, apart from of course, *illegitimacy.* This still caused shock horror with everybody and to an extent still does to this day in some quarters, especially amongst older people. So mother, just a child herself, had a baby and was in the clutches of a mother who thankfully had her fifth and last child, (by the third husband) at much the same time. She, giving birth at forty seven, was exceptional even in those days and the baby was perfect.

She had a beautiful blond baby girl, Mother's half sister. So Grandma was able to keep her daughter Annie and baby at home, *and hope*. She hoped and prayed that the story of having twins would fool most of the populace. To my Mothers' credit, she refused to give her daughter up to be brought up by *her* mother. She was given a very hard time for this and was forced to live in London with her married sister for a while.

Grandma punished her considerably with both mental and physical cruelty. She had caused the face saving plan to fall apart. Grandma could have retained at least *some* of her waning status, after marrying the man she did.

After a break in South London with her sister Barbara and her husband Richard, she felt that the time had come for her to give her sister and family, their privacy back— they had children as well. Also quiet nights without a young baby crying would have been welcome. She had no option, but to return to her home. So she returned to Malvern with the baby and stayed with her Mother and step Father once more, as things had again quietened down.

Barbara, her sister—must have helped her a lot as she was such a young mother. She was so immature and up to then, hadn't lived away from home. It must have been a shock to a teenager, trying to cope with a child—there was no help as there is today. No wonder she and her sister were so close throughout their lives. When she went back to Malvern, it was a tempestuous existence for Mother, constant rows broke out.

Time passed and eventually, my mother was to meet and fall in love with a golden haired professional soldier.

He was a gymnast, and a very athletic one who competed for the Army. He specialised in the Pommel Vault and the Still Rings and he also trained his men in physical education. He looked like a blond God. He was muscled, very strong and good looking but also a generous and kind natured man. Eventually he was seconded to the Royal Air Force to assist with important war work. When I was very young, at about the age of six, I remember seeing a photograph of him shaking hands with General Montgomery so I guess he was a skilled soldier. He was very smitten with Mother and he was good to her daughter as well. They were married, quietly without a fuss and held the reception at her Mother's house.

The financial assistance ceased from Daphne's father—which was only to be expected of course. But the Second World War intervened and the new handsome husband left to fight as an officer, along with all the other able bodied young men to France.

Time passed and there was a spell of calm, but before long the distance and the circumstances, were to cause much misery in the lives of many marriages.

Once again, mother and her little one were living with her married older sister in South London. By then, Daphne was at Boarding school on the Kent coast. Mother was doing war effort at Woolwich Arsenal. Equipped with a hard hat for the raids with a butterfly painted on it, she looked adorable in her dungarees.

She started out working on machines as many girls did. Unbelievably, there was a strike, even in Wartime. Mother refused to strike and was called a 'Bloody Blackleg'. She would not down tools. A large man armed with a spanner advanced on her brandishing it. She must have been somewhat alarmed, being only five feet tall and seven stone.

Her bravery was noticed and she was quickly taken off the machines and put in the wages office. It was a much more suitable occupation for a petite and intelligent girl. She worked out the overtime wages for the staff's entitlement.

The boss in her department was casting a beady eye on her, she was brave and smart. She was also lonely. Young lonely girls felt the temptations that loneliness can bring, with the ever present fear, that Hitler could end life as they knew it.

Various escapades and fun presented itself. When she had days off, she and the other office friends would go out as a little group, in the company of the *good looking* Boss. Brown eyed and dashing, he was a fascinating man, also educated and charming.

Chapter Seven

The work location was dangerous. The Arsenal was a natural target for the bombers, who flew up the Thames and homed in above it. It was only a matter of time before it was hit.

The wages group formed friendships, and picnics were held in fields by the river in the sun. It was a glorious summer that year.

Alas, the unimaginable happened. Mother found herself pregnant once more. There was no pregnancy protection, no legitimate abortion, how could you expect a pretty girl to be loyal when temptation was all around? Many *were* loyal, many weren't—how many women passed off babies as the husbands' in those days? My mother couldn't however. Her husband was in France.

She, at that moment, destroyed the lives of her two girls.

Her family, in Malvern, had by then, got the small town to settle down and talk about someone else.

Her husband must have been broken hearted when told. He stopped sending money home. He was a junior officer and considered a gentleman. They didn't have to send money like the other ranks, so he didn't. Why should he? He probably thought, let her starve. There was only the means test to procure extra funds for the family and she would never have taken that. She was plunged into hell and penury.

I have to say, she **was** foolish—nevertheless, it is very easy to become pregnant, there were no modern benefits, and you know the old saying, '*one shouldn't throw stones.*' It also takes two.

The family, comprising a nine year old and a pregnant Mother, had to manage as best they could. Daphne was away at boarding school. I am pretty certain that *my* father assisted mother with some financial help, he was a kind man and must have worried a great deal about her. She didn't live as badly as she could have if she had nothing.

I never officially knew him however. I just surmised that he was my Dad, because of his actions when I was a child. He was very gentle and used to cuddle me a lot when he visited us. He came down several times to Malvern years later. He was still living in Woolwich, looking after his elderly Mum.

Whilst working at Woolwich Arsenal, mother wasn't surprised when the factory was bombed. She was shocked though. She said the rats were seen leaving in droves. The arsenal was obviously at great risk remaining in London, as now it was a prime target for the bombers. It was decided that part of the arsenal be quietly moved in 1941, to Blackpole (originally the old Cadbury's factory), a large establishment in Worcester. All very *hush hush*—but it enabled Mother to live once more in Malvern, where of course I was born, that same year.

Mum did seem to have a childlike need to return to her Mother, apart from the fact that life must have been very difficult with the buzz bombs in South London, not to mention the pregnancy. Her mother could also be delightful company sometimes; she loved music, sang well and was well read. After the shocking sights of London, Malvern must have seemed a haven of peace and there was an abundance of food at her mother's house compared with what she would have been able to get staying with her sister in South London. She told me many tales of scary happenings throughout her time of travelling to work in the London black out, *I am a brave person* but some of the happenings that befell Mum were creepy.

She once, on her way to work, saw the body of a woman draped over telegraph wires and there was a large crater in the road. They all had to get off the bus, getting another one further on. When I was a child, we had a huge piece of shrapnel which she had picked up. It was in our glass cabinet. *Shrapnel was exploded bomb,* it was sharp and heavy. Times may have been 'matey' but they were horrific too. So returning to Malvern must have been a great relief. There were no bombs there.

I was born at my Grandmother's house and eventually Mother returned to work at Blackpole. I was minded by Grandma who loved babies fortunately. Daphne was at Boarding School in Kent, but when Mother found out that German fliers were unloading their last bombs before crossing the channel and little Daphne was spending a lot of time under the stairs at her school; she was immediately fetched back to Malvern. She eventually attended a sweet little Convent School at Malvern Link, an area a few miles away.

She was an innocent little girl who knew no bad words; her upbringing had been gentle and refined. Despite the horrendous rows that were between her Mother and Grandma, she never heard or witnessed them, neither did I as a child.

Before the convent school, she spent a short time at a school called Mill Lane. It was a council school and contained children from all walks of life.

One day, the little Daphne saw 'S H I T' written by some rascal on the blackboard. As the teacher came in to class, my sister put up her hand and asked, "What is S. H. one T?" The teacher went ballistic, she thought my sister knew and was being facetious. My sister genuinely didn't. She had never heard that word. She was marched to the front and caned. When she got home, she tearfully told all. Mother and Grandma explained, she wasn't to know, but it was a naughty word. Then they went to the school and took her away. It was pretty obvious that a shy, nervous little girl like her was to be believed in such matters. However in a way, it turned out to be a good thing, as the next school was excellent.

Grandma adored little babies, and with my sister being at school most of the time, she could handle me easily. Each evening after a long hard day and a train ride home, Mum would bathe and feed tea to me. We had our own room, the attic—where we lived.

The autumn supply of apples had been stored up there in the recent past. The room smelled lovely and 'appley' . . . although austere with a sky light (Dormer windows, not being invented at that time). I was fine with it however, as we were <u>all</u> there and not just me. I do remember the night-light flickering and the sooty patch on the sloping ceiling above it.

I was a pretty brown eyed baby with country rosy cheeks and loved by all. Mother however, was not loved and frequent rows broke out, probably about her husband. There was no divorce but he didn't return.

One very big row culminated with us all being thrown out. Goodness knows what happened, but I remember sitting on a case outside, waiting for the taxi.

I went to one family and my sister to another. Hers' was an elderly couple who had an upholstery business— Fred and Fanny Frost; they were very fond and kind to her. The folk Mum and I went to are a mystery to me, as I was very small.

Chapter Eight

That was one of many *ejections* from Grandmother's place. Even so, we must have eventually returned yet again, maybe Mother knew she was difficult and begged to go back.

When I was four, we were certainly there. I remember living at Grandma's and deciding to hold my own flag day. I had seen people with tins and trays of little Union Jack flags with pins, collecting for the disabled Servicemen. I thought that was a super idea as I knew money bought treats. I made my own little flags and coloured them with my pencils—attaching them to pins. I tied a tin tray around my neck with string and off I went when no one was looking, across the Green and positioned myself outside the bakers. With my empty *jam jar* at the ready, some people gave me pennies and I even had a three penny bit, they must have seen the funny side. Grandma did not—someone went across to her house and said "Have you seen what your Granddaughter's up to on the Green?" So another idea bit the dust.

I seemed to take to selling quite naturally, I became rather good at it later in my life.

There must have been yet another row, as we were sent off again, but this time to a rented Victorian place at the base of the hills. This house was OLD. It was up at the top of an old steep road called Pump Street. It was practically on the hills. There must have been an old pump for the area there once upon a time. I shouldn't have liked carrying a bucket down or up that street, for it was terribly steep. There was an old dairy opposite (I recall it being called Ansteys'dairy)—this was over seventy years ago though. I wouldn't go there unless my Mummy forced me as it smelled awfully of sour milk. The poor horses that must have pulled carts and floats along to that dairy in the olden days, must have suffered, the street was directly on the side of the hill. Mother used to get us cream there.

The ground floor flat was sub-let illegally by the upstairs tenant, a nervous soul named Nora. We nicknamed the poor thing 'Nervy Nora'. Her son was a lawyer so she should have known better than to sub-let to us. But for a while, we were happy there because we had peace. Mother gave up working in Worcester and got a job in Malvern Town, not too far away. Probably Nora minded me when I wasn't at my first little 'infants' school. I wonder why Nora was alone. She could have lost her husband in the war but I never knew her story. The war cruelly took away so many men and left women single. In Malvern, next door to my Grandmother—the family lost two sons in submarines; it is dreadful what people went through. I would have gone around the bend, I'm sure.

My first little infant's school was totally charming. The headmistress was so kind. She firmly believed that children should first develop their drawing and painting skills before reading. She taught me to love the Arts and I have been painting ever since. Trouble was, when I eventually went to another school down near Grandma's, the teacher had me out at the front to be laughed at, I was so backward compared to the others. The old methods of teaching involved a lot of humiliation but I survived it. We were all caned regularly, we weren't especially naughty—we probably spoke a bit too much, we were supposed to sit quietly in those days. Grandma taught me to read in about a fortnight however. I was old enough to make light work of it. Grandma told me that she once went to a Dame School in the country when she was a child. They had slates. I remember forever making blots from the nibs of the 'dip in inkwell' pens of the day. It was positively prehistoric then. I understand that pens are going out of fashion now, along with paper. It is staggering to see the youngsters working on their computers, their fingers fly. Wouldn't I have loved a computer when I was young, fantastic . . . there is no need for ignorance now; it is all there at the touch of a mouse or screen.

The house called 'Bay Tree' in Pump Street was large, cold but stylish with an open fire. It had a veranda.

We had few possessions in those days, but I remember us making a rag rug with a little hooking device, we hooked bits of cloth through little holes. It was great fun to a small child. The final effect was sweet, with areas so obviously done by children, but it went in front of the fire and we were proud. The furniture was orange boxes covered with bits of chintz, plus the odd *monstrosity* left in the place before we came because it was too heavy to move Mother did get us two arm chairs however, she and Daphne sat on them and I had a cushion on the rug before the fire. The Victorians sure did love their massive sideboards and heavy old items in dark wood. Some were too heavy to lift and rooms were made with high ceilings and long walls which made the fitting of them possible. I suppose the 'upper classes' had servants to help each other with the moving process of these colossal pieces, they would have been ordered to clean behind them in case of spiders webs—no poking the vacuum pipe behind and sucking the dust out. How the poor things must have slaved in the large houses in those days. They weren't all Stately Homes with lots of staff; those are just the subject matter of television films. The usual houses owned by Dentists or Business people, were time consuming enough to run for the families who lived in them. They had to cook and sew for the family as well—it must have been a pretty thankless existence. But, my sympathy was really for the servants of the smaller houses. The owners would have only been able to afford a couple of 'dog's bodies' to do it all. Most jobs would have entailed the poor looking after the rich—other than that, a shop assistant would have been the common role. Girls got very little time off, when they did, there was a strict code of conduct, you couldn't dress or act above your station.

We as a family should have had a better standard of living; Grandma didn't help us cope despite her thousands in the bank. I can remember my Mother handing over her coupons to Grandma when she allowed us some eggs from her many chickens; she was mean and un-motherly in every way. Thank heavens that the genes haven't been handed down to the modern generation, all my children love each other a great deal. Could it be that Grandma blamed Mother in some way for the death of her husband? I wish I knew how she thought—I was just a small child.

When we were at 'Bay Tree' we were given a little tabby kitten, but when we were discovered by the owner, we had to go again . . . the kitty was left with the lady upstairs who fortunately, wasn't ejected.

The lower flat, ours—was awfully damp though, we had a spring running through the cellar and when the rains came it got flooded and things floated around down there, bumping into walls. We used to call it our ghost, but I wasn't afraid. I still to this day, have a lovely copper kettle that came from the cellar. Doubtless someone got fed up cleaning it.

We even got snowed in. It was the winter of 1947. The weather was fierce but my sister and I had gone onto the hills (over the road was a path) and foolishly I left my toy bear 'Winnie the Pooh', under a bush in the snow. I couldn't sleep without it, so my poor sister had to retrace our steps and try to locate it. She found it and I adored my big sister even more, if that was possible. When the snow first came, our front door had to be dug out, exciting stuff for a little child. We have suffered terrible winters since then of course but that one was a classic and services were rather basic in those days. That winter really did seem to go on interminably. It was a terrible year for everyone, as the snow closed everything down nationally. Lots of poor animals died in the drifts, it was dreadful for the farmers especially.

Chapter Nine

After our illicit renting had been discovered, the stress must have been terrible for Mother. We ended up going back down to Grandma's house which I loved, as it had an enormous garden. There was also a little white smooth haired terrier called Patch.

Patch belonged to Grandma's youngest daughter. She often made Patch yelp when she fiddled with his paws. I suffered at her hands too. She chased me with a long worm dangling, which she said she was going to put down my neck. To this day, I don't like them. Anything legless that slithers, yuck. My screams were deafening as I thundered into the house with Jane in pursuit. At least Grandma told her off. Since then, I have been the world's worst gardener. If I dig a worm up, I have to jump back and wait for it to go back down . . . It makes planting anything a very long process.

As a very small girl, I didn't know what was going on. The rows that were occurring were well away from my little ears. They could have been partly due to Grandma's youngest daughter Jane, she was mean at times. I expect she thought that I stole some of the attention away from her. She hated me playing with her dog, I heard her complaining about it but it didn't get her anywhere.

I loved the dog, the garden and the step Grandfather. I remember his 'Players' cigarettes and his manly smell. He didn't have a beard, and apart from the slight smell of cigarettes, he always smelled fragrant. He was very sweet to me and also cuddly, when I was in need of a father or a male figure, to love. I remember watching him shaving and his dabbing soap on my cheek, he always made me laugh. He was always so fresh and clean and fragrant. He wasn't terribly tall, but a lot of shorter men seem to have so much more personality and a greater sense of humour. I truly loved him.

I even loved Grandma. As I was so young, I didn't see the half. She got her revenge though, by mentally torturing my Mother. She was always threatening her with the alarming threat, that she would tell *me* the truth.

I remember a dreadful fight between them, when I was eleven years old. I could never work out what was so serious that they would attack each other. I eventually found out, but when I was quite grown up and Mother had passed away.

She must have had a lifetime of punishment for her weakness when so young. How sad. If only she had found the courage to tell me. I loved her and it wouldn't have made an iota of difference.

I have always been rather unconventional and understanding of human weakness, anyway. I have also believed throughout my life, that secrets are best revealed. Small children can adjust to them gradually though life and shocks are avoided. I have observed that children understand much more than people realise anyway. They pick up on atmosphere instantly, it is very hard to fool kids.

This brings me to say and by the way, this is purely a personal opinion—you may not agree. Some people, *(it can apply to either sex, loads of men bring up the children in today's society)* who haven't revealed the injustices that befell them during the marriage; find that when the kids reach their teens, they are tempted to get in touch with the missing parent. Being unaware of the truth of the broken marriage, many swap loyalties and go over to the other previously indifferent or cruel parent; breaking the heart of the parent who raised them—often with great sacrifice, to adulthood.

It is so easy to manipulate the youngster and get revenge on the mum or dad who did all the loving, caring and growing-up of the child. The reason is often that the Mother hid the truth about the Father, when they were little. This can end up mighty dangerous for the innocent partner. I have known more than one individual who have had their hearts broken this way. The crafty ex—partner; capitalises on the youngster's ignorance of the true facts and often buys them with financial treats.

My own children knew that my husband treated me dreadfully. I am not saying that a partner, who commits adultery, should lose the love of their children. That would be positively Victorian. Men who have been sadistic to their wives (and there are plenty), are quite another matter.

I am sad about the way children are often used as tools to spite the other partner. A member of my own family was punished by his wife and made to lose his children, by a false accusation. It was eventually proved without a shadow of doubt that it was a 'set up', he never did anything wrong. His wife just did not want him anymore. He has spent years suffering. What happened to him is so evil that I would be reduced to a weepy wreck if I wrote it here. It would reduce you to a very depressed person too—there is no end to the evil that some women can devise, especially with the assistance of their mothers.

Chapter Ten

This is intended to be an uplifting account of my existence, I have now a wonderful happening to relate.

After a while, my step Grandfather who knew a man on the council, managed to get us a prefab. They were new, a perfect answer to the homeless after the war. We got one that was built to house the incoming scientists who were going to work at the R.R.E. (Royal Radar Establishment, soon to become Ministry of Defence). Mother was able to get a job there as she was brainy and useful. There was a bonus; she could walk to work thus saving fares.

The prefab was the last word in modernity. We had a fitted bathroom, a fitted kitchen, a refrigerator and even a washing machine of sorts, all installed behind matching doors. There was no gas but we liked electricity. We were used to a big copper that used to heat up the bath water at Grandma's place. It groaned and creaked and used to terrify me. Also we had a copper that was for boiling the clothes at Grandma's. There was a scrubbing board and a stick, all grey and smooth for poking the sheets and towels when they were boiling. Washing day was a big deal on a Monday, with cold meat and 'bubble and squeak' for lunch. In our new prefab, we could throw our towels and bits and bobs in anytime and the washing was easy. We three walked on air, we were so happy.

We were the envy of everyone; our prefab didn't even feel small as we were just three females and petite, Mother being five feet tall and my sister only five foot four and me an eight year old. We even had room for a piano, an upright of course—goodness knows where it came from, maybe from financial assistance that Mother received from my secret father . . . but it was a very good make.

Mother being quite a pianist, was offered a job in a band. She knew the trumpeter through work, he got her the job. She had a ball. Drinks were lined up for her on top of the band's piano like in a film. She was able to wear pretty clothes and feel feminine. She played at the country 'hops'. I expect every village dance hall had a piano in those days. It must have been wonderful for her after what she had been through, and the extra money would have been useful.

The colour theme of the prefab was rust red, with a big rust red 'Axminster' carpet and red and white curtains. It looked lovely with the white walls and the dark furniture. She had good taste and there was always a glass vase of red dahlias, or some other colourful flowers from our huge garden. We had loads of trees and it was heaven for a little girl. It was a happy ending to a difficult start.

We even managed a holiday in St. Ives, before we moved in. Mother and we two girls, stayed in a hotel. My father again I expect.

The man I have to assume was my father was not poor and came to visit us at the prefab, dangling me on his knee. How I wish he had been able to marry Mum, he was a lovely man. He used to call me 'Anna Powerovsky' (a derivation of Mother's married name) as I ballet danced. He seemed fond of me, to my childish eyes. Mother would get me to don my 'tutu' and ballet shoes. I wonder what eventually became of this gorgeous person. When he took her out to dinner, she would wear powder and lipstick and as she kissed me goodnight, the scent of her would linger in my bedroom, she was so girlish and happy, his visits stripped years off her and she was carefree again. I even remember the 'Ponds' makeup that she used and the scent of it. The supplies of aids for beauty were rather limited in those post war times but she certainly made a great impression on me.

Hoddy, as I called him, real surname Hodson—had a Grandmother who had been Egyptian. That accounted for his dark eyes and slightly olive complexion. Every little girl needs to know who her father is, we definitely require 'roots'—*despite some of them being a big disappointment.* I would certainly have loved to know for certain, but Mother refused to say. I suppose he *may* have been married . . . alas. Perhaps she might have thought that one day I would try to find him and upset his wife, assuming he had one. I could even have step-brothers or sisters, imagine what a thrill that would be. My children and I have always been brunettes with dark eyes; maybe that is the foreign blood. I wear a Nefertiti pendant around my neck constantly as homage to my *possible* father. Maybe it is silly, but it pleases me.

I do think my mother would have eventually driven him mad, if they had been together. She was difficult to live with, but maybe with the right person who could stay and always be there . . . ?

One day I heard Mother moaning to Daphne, that the immersion heater was gobbling up all our money. Our electricity bills were phenomenal.

A firm of local soft fruit growers was advertising for pickers. I decided as a surprise, to have a go at it but

I didn't tell anyone. I earned quite a bit towards that electricity bill. Mum was thrilled and surprised that I set off to do it all on my own as I was only nine. Those little berries are the very devil to pick, it helped that I was short. How a tall person would cope I can't imagine.

Another scheme I devised was to pick the primroses from our local and quite nearby railway bank. It was covered with them. In those days, steam trains were in use, they were majestic and scary to a small girl as they thundered past up above me. It was rather a shame that I wasn't a 'train-spotting' boy; I would have been spoilt for choice as we had very interesting old trains passing not far away from our house. They weren't super fast Expresses, one looked like a coffee pot and we christened it such. The letters on the side were the L.M.S. and a bigger and more spectacular one was sporting a G.W.R. on it. They chuffed by on their way to the tunnel which took them through the hills to Herefordshire and Wales. I used to wave to them and people waved back, like in the Railway Children. It was fun and not annoying at all having trains so close. They didn't put me off my picking primroses though and I picked baskets full but I did keep my head down, as a girl on the bank would have been illegal. I tied them up surrounded by leaves, and with the green wool around them, they made pretty bunches. They didn't get dirty as one would imagine being on the railway bank, they nestled beneath brambles which were another source of joy when autumn came. My Mother made us apple and blackberry pies from the scrumped apples I got whilst riding past them, as they hung over the fences in the orchards. The black berries after a good rinse were succulent and easy to obtain. I traipsed along all the prefabs and sold my goodies to the amused housewives.

Later in the season, I sold bunches of rhubarb which grew in profusion in our back vegetable garden. I loved being entrepreneurial. When Christmas came around, I also visited all the big grand detached houses the other side of the road with my friend, singing carols and the residents paid up royally. Christmas was too good a chance to miss and our little voices trilling some of the prettier carols must have been sweet. We were nine or ten but nerves didn't seem to assail us—*there was only one problem though*. We did some of our best singing outside one of the biggest houses. The maid came to the door and informed us that it was the local deaf and dumb home. Well you can't win them all . . .

All my earnings went to Mother. She must have smiled sometimes, but it was real money in those days. I even used my chestnut pony Shandy, to give short rides on at church fetes. The poor old church didn't get much, three quarters went to Mum. I doubt if I'll ever get to heaven.

But Life was fun and challenging and in the main, wonderful.

Chapter Eleven

Mother didn't risk boyfriends. Maybe she was still in love with my father. I do not know, but she removed her husband from the doorstep when he came to patch things up. In retrospect now, I have great sympathy for him. His was a very raw deal after all. However, she wasn't risking the happiness of her little family. I was a very contented little girl.

Life seems to ensure that we can't *ride the crest of the wave* for keeps. For, when I reached my teenage years, poor Mother reached the 'change of life'.

There was no H.R.T. in those days and it seemed to bring about a great deterioration in her mental health. She became very excitable and unreasonable. She suffered terrible tantrums and made my life hell. She was the 'teenager' . . . I became the mother. I had to do nearly everything in the house and the shopping. I grew up in a hurry, I had to.

I think maybe part of the mood swings and trouble with my Mum, apart from the obvious diminishing of her oestrogen, was that my sister had married and lived away in London. She adored her and just tolerated me. I was the child that caused her to suffer the most. For most of my life she left me to more or less get on with it.

Thankfully I had Shandy and was out most of the time. There was no excuse for *my* birth in her mind, it was purely her fault. Although not married, she was so young when she conceived my sister, it was excusable. I could go on to quote many neglectful happenings, this would be wrong of me though. Many of us do not get all the support that we deserve, when young. I just compensated for it, by being very caring with my own children.

My teenage years were not filled with sex, drugs and rock 'n' roll. Malvern was quiet—too quiet. A big night out was gathering at Youth Club, or outside the chip shop, for meeting friends.

Sometimes I rode my horse to hunt meets. There were two main hunts, the Croome and the North Ledbury. I rode out in all weathers, just for peace and for the joy of seeing countryside normally unreachable, because of hedges and gates.

We didn't usually make a kill and I don't remember the Master or Whipper In, digging the fox out when he'd gone to earth. When we did manage to catch one, I didn't watch the gory bits, but there was a gruesome melee as the hounds pounced on the poor victim. As a girl, I just did not see the cruelty of it. I thought that foxes were vermin. They certainly removed the heads from our Rhode Island Red chickens. My fresh egg collection came to a sudden halt. I always and still do, think that stag hunting is savage. Those poor creatures, they don't hurt anybody. I knew a woman who had a terrified stag being pursued by hounds, crash through her patio windows—not seeing them in its panic. This was some years ago. I hope and assume it no longer takes place but I fear it does in Devon. How on earth can folk justify causing such terror in modern enlightened times? Now that I am grown up, I wouldn't hunt any creature to kill it, just to capture it on film—that is real fun.

My tireless chestnut had three fawn socks and one white one which was considered lucky. With his blond mane and tail and lovely disposition, he grew up with me. He was mine when he was five years old and he reached the grand old age of forty five. He had every lucky horsey quirk that a horse could have.

Apart from having one white sock, he had a double crown, and a white chin (called a snip). There was an old country saying, 'One white sock buy him, two white socks try him, three white socks doubt him, four white socks, do without him.' There were many silly sayings about horses when I was a child, there were many silly *and cruel* horse practises as well.

People have learned so much more about animals now, thank heavens. Now 'Breaking Them In' tends to be called 'Backing them'—a much kinder expression. One certainly does not want to BREAK the Spirit of a young horse. *Neither, does one want to eat them.*

Those who eat horse meat should be ashamed. It is quite unnecessary. Don't they realise that without the invaluable help horses have given us through the centuries, we would still be primitive. They are the one creature who has advanced civilisation beyond all others, dogs are wonderful and truly useful apart from being 'Man's Best Friend', but you cannot ride dogs. It is true that they can be driven in front of a sleigh and are of great benefit in cold climates; horses lead the usefulness stakes though. What would the world have done without horses before cars were invented? There is no need to breed them for the table. It is a terrible sin. To eat something so easily domesticated as a horse or a dog, will cause something hideous to happen. What goes around comes around.

Cows are perfectly easily bred for the *table*, sad though it is—speaking as a vegetarian, but they can't be ridden and used to pull things. If people *must* eat meat—let it not be horses. I used to pass a field of piebald ponies bred by Gypsies. They were travellers really, not true gypsies of Romany descent. They traded them as a valuable commodity for the table. It is BIG hidden money. Tax free and enabling these people to make the fortunes that they always have. This 'black' money helps give them the fantastic lifestyle they enjoy. They are very affluent and the adult's interest in horse flesh is purely financial.

My little horse at 14 hands 2 inches, (a 'hand' was considered about four inches then), was just the right size for me. He was roan coloured (dark red), more than chestnut. He was a gelding and gelded rather late. He would round up other horses—especially mares—whenever he had the chance. He thought he was a stallion. He had a thick neck and long mane and tail. He was an intelligent animal and I adored him. He had a lot of Arab in him and was a spritely and comfortable ride, with short strides. This was ideal for a small person. I had many offers to sell him, but I never would.

When he rested and lay down, I used to lie in his legs with my head on his stomach. I would secure him in the paddock at the back of our prefab. He would often lie down to take the weight off his hooves. Our tabby cat 'Oofy' (short for 'Who flung dung', a Chinese name) would lie on him too. The three of us must have looked very peaceful and quite sweet.

He never kicked or nipped me, or was impatient with a little girl, who must have irritated him often. His only fault was that he often forgot that he was a horse and not a dog. When I brought him home to graze the two large lawns, to save the mowing, he would come into the kitchen through the back door and steal fruit from the bowl on the kitchen table. How he didn't go through the floorboards I will never know.

We had imitation wood patterned linoleum too and his hooves didn't damage it. It must have been tough quality. He also used to chomp on the rose bushes and I had a photo of him for years, which I have now lost, with a rose hanging out of the side of his mouth and a guilty look on his face. I wish that I could find this photograph. He looked so like a guilty school boy.

I did not go to pony club, they were formal types there and snobby in my consideration. Anyway, I didn't have the immaculate riding clothes. My riding jacket was creeping up my arms. Mum couldn't afford new stuff for me. I was perfectly happy playing with him, hacking around the woods and commons. Although we won the odd rosette for gymkhana events, I did not enjoy the usual discipline of structured horse management. We were just two youngsters growing up together. I must have done something right; he lived so much longer than most horses do. Forty five human years for a horse is very rare.

All my friends and family had a go on him, he was very patient. I used to make Mother laugh by sitting backwards and jumping little jumps in the paddock.

When I eventually moved to London, we sold him to a charming little woman, who I recall was a retired School Teacher. She was rather old and quaintly Victorian, but she was a dear little lady who still rode well. She was gentle and loved him. When she became too old to ride, she passed him on to another friend who really loved him too and taught her little girl to ride on him.

Chapter Twelve

We always knew exactly what became of him and knew that his life would always be secure and happy.

Before then, we rode on the hills when they seemed deserted. It was a lovely vast and empty kind of loneliness, I was in my own world and it was heaven. Sir Edward Elgar, when he was alive, who was born and lived in Worcestershire, had walked them regularly in the past. He was certainly inspired by them. Some of the themes in his great works reflect the magic.

Cynics might say 'a hill is just a hill'. I disagree. Malvern Hills are incredibly beautiful in a gentle way. I knew them backwards. I knew where little springs popped out through rocks that were off the normal paths. Sometimes in windy weather, I loved to lie on the grass and watch the quaking grasses rippling in the breezes. It was like velvet trembling, I do not know what type of wild grass it was—not being a botanist. It was lovely though and a soft brown in colour, I expect that was the grasses being in seed. In those days, the hill 'Conservators' (the body who protect them) were pretty casual, there were few signs and rules, I could go anywhere. I am sure horses would not be allowed to meander all over them today. The air was pure and wonderful and the solitude would help me unscramble my mind, home life was rather chaotic.

I was a solitary girl, with just Shandy for company, I needed no other. I was given my horse when I was eight and he went like the wind. I used to sit on the sofa arm and pretend to ride—this was o.k. at four, but I was a bit larger and Mother could see that I spent my life dreaming of horses. So somehow she managed to get me one. Some of my most joyous times were riding him bare backed, flying along trying to beat the steam trains as they roared along towards Herefordshire, it was a truly great place to grow up.

I remember when I first saw him. Mother and friend, drove me to a small country village outside Malvern. He was tied to a flowering apple tree and his summer coat gleamed in the spring sun. It was love at first sight and a present of a little snaffle bridle and a felt saddle complete with girth and stirrups were mine too.

We saddled him up and I hacked him back seven miles to home. I wish I could have seen my face, I grinned from ear to ear, but I was the wrong side of it. We bonded immediately. Video cameras were not readily owned by all then, especially people like us. A video of the time I first saw him, would have been something great to show my kids. I think Shandy, my immediate family and my children, were my only real intense loves for life. Maybe my cat too, he was exceptional come to think of it. More of him later.

It is expensive feeding and maintaining horses. I taught riding by buying a cheap little New Forest, bay filly and backing her. She cost so little that my saved pocket money could afford her.

When I first got her, she had a curly mane and tail, she was so young. A local chap who was driving in that area picked her up and put her into his van. He was naughty, but I am glad, as he sold her to me. I called her Sherry. Riding lessons were always terribly expensive.

Several young daughters belonging to the local folk persuaded their Mothers to let them have half priced lessons, and I learned how to teach others. I also built savings for the bad weather to come, when rugs and hay were needed. It was a good job I had been originally well taught by Pam, she lived near us and was very horsey.

Pam was a true friend. She lived in a little black and white cottage of great age. Her Father and Mother hung up a 'Flitch' (a side of bacon) from a hook in the kitchen ceiling. The cottage was tiny, cluttered and dark. It had stood there for many hundreds of years. Going into it was a step back into history and it would be listed now.

It was with Pam and her father that I used to go and help with the haymaking. I rode in an old fashioned dray—a horse drawn receptacle with a board at the front that your feet rested on and which had separate wheels under it. When it turned a corner it was a strange sensation, my feet went first and my body followed. I was allowed to have a go at driving the horse pulling it, what a thrill. We forked up hay with pitch forks into it, how many people still remember doing that I wonder? This was a proper Thomas Hardy moment. Maybe folk still use drays, but they would now be pulled by tractor.

Pam was strong and stocky. She was a real country girl and a wonderful horse woman.

Pam became a real friend. She was responsible for giving me my first lacy blue suspender belt. I was fourteen and going to my first grown up dance. I had never had anything lovely to wear since my silk baby dresses which mother smocked, but I never really noticed them as I was a baby. I tended to live in jodhpurs or jeans, apart from my school uniform of course. I had never wanted dresses.

This first dance dress was strapless, with a little Bolero. It was pale yellow and taffeta. In those days, they were worn below the knee, but they swirled out when we spun around.

The dance was at the boys college, and we danced the evening away with Reels and Scottish dances with my borrowed dress (Pam again) flying, and feeling very adult in my new underwear and nylons.

My friend Pam has passed away now but I will always be grateful to her for the kindness she gave to me. She even made me her bridesmaid when she rode to her wedding on a white horse.

She taught me 'Dog Latin and Back Slang' a way of speaking, that *grownups can't generally understand*. We gabbled away and the adults tried to figure it out, it was great fun. She really understood and was kind to a little girl who ate, drank and slept horses.

As I got older and took an interest in the local Gazette, the towns' parochial attitudes, got me down.

My girl friend and I were stopped by a policeman for riding two on a bike and we ended up in court. Mother had to take a day off work and it made the papers . . . we got *conditional* discharges. I felt like a criminal and I was only 12. I suppose they didn't have enough crime in Malvern so Sue and I were useful for their crime sheets.

We also had several experiences of men exposing themselves to us, and once we enabled the law to catch a well known and dangerous paedophile.

We two girls, my friend Sylvia and I, were up a horse chestnut tree on the local common. Before the war, it had been a huge golf course. This common was well off the beaten track, at the less populated end of Malvern.

An old guy wearing a dog collar and leading his bicycle, stopped underneath the tree and looking up at us—two pretty little girls in shorts, suggested that we go to "romp" on the little mound in the adjoining part of the common. We knew that was very suspicious, we didn't go much on the 'Romping' bit. There was a big branch separating us from him by reason of a pointed metal railing that would be between us if we moved along it. We immediately scrambled along it out of his reach. Swinging down a smaller branch, we landed nimbly onto the inaccessible side of the fence and safety. We took off as fast as our legs could carry us. As luck would have it, two people were walking their dog over near the railway line on the other side of the common and witnessed it all. We told my Mum what happened and the people came up and verified it too, they must have known where I lived. When the police were called, they caught the bloke, he had obviously offended before as he vanished and a good thing too. We were about nine at the time.

The next happening was when I was twelve years old. I had returned my pony to his field, down a narrow lane. I would have to return along it to get to the main road and wait for a bus to take me the three miles home. It was early evening and I was in the heart of real country. To my horror, a farm worker who lived in a cottage at the top of the lane was standing there exposing himself. As I advanced toward him, he stretched his arms out to catch me. The lane was just wide enough for a tractor to drive along it and the big farm where he worked was at the other end. I didn't let him see me looking at his open trousers. I had the presence of mind to call out to him 'What time is it?' and as he instinctively looked down at his watch. I took my chance, shouting 'Goodness, Mum will skin me alive.' I started running, swinging the bridle, just missing his face, the metal 'bit' swished through the air at speed. I dodged under his arm and ran like hell. As I reached the larger lane which led to the main road, a miracle happened. A passing van, driven by the local butcher doing deliveries, saw me running. He knew me and must have seen my desperate face. He stopped and picked me up and drove me home. I told him the story as we were on our way, and he dropped me at Mums. This time, because the *employe*r of the farmhand said that he was a good worker, he wasn't prosecuted. I was accused of 'Romancing' by the Police.

I felt very cross about that because if he had caught me, goodness knows what would have happened. I was really accused of lying. The girl who also kept her pony in that field was a doctor's daughter, called Janet. Mother went to her father's house and told him what had happened and her pony was also removed to a safer place. It would seem that unless someone had actually witnessed the event, or I had been found raped and murdered, the local police made no effort to prove anything. I had previously seen the man lying under his van supposedly mending it, with his equipment showing through the front of his overalls (*I don't mean his spanner either*). At the time, my older girl friend June, who was temporarily staying at our house, was riding up behind me on Shandy. We were delivering him back to his field in the early evening. We innocently thought that it was a mistake and he would have been embarrassed had he known. Even June, *who was several years older than me, and working,* was fooled. **He was a rampant pervert and dangerous.** June backed up my story but still nothing was done about him.

It was terribly humiliating and embarrassing when a policeman asked me what I saw, there was no woman police officer to help my blushes. I blurted out 'what do you think?' This probably didn't help me much. I think that one of the senior police in that constabulary must have had some strange issues going on. Why else were we ignored? How could his employer the farmer, who said that he was a good worker, have mattered a jot. Why wasn't June, my witness believed? I was not yet a teenager and my experiences were so shocking. It is no wonder that many 'straight' girls grow up to *'bat for the other side'*.

Chapter Thirteen

I remember a lovely Italian girl who was living with her partner in a bedsit, in my house. She said that her father used to threaten her with the Mafia, unless she let him interfere with her, from twelve years on. Her partner Angela had her kitten put outside on the window ledge, until her father had finished with her, she knew he would push it off if she complained, and they were high up in flats. These aren't isolated incidents.

One should always believe a child and remember that a large percentage of paedophiles are women. It is stated by the 'Bureau of Statistics' that 30% are. I can only think sadly, that when the poor little child goes to her mother to complain about Daddy, the mother is one of two things, **an accomplice** or afraid to have to exist without him, so she would rather sacrifice her child. I guess that she would know that her life style would change if she told the police, but why would she want a life style like that anyway? He couldn't love his wife if he sexually desired her child could he?

These weak creatures that call themselves 'mothers' need punishing more than the men, they should know better, they carried the child for nine months. I personally think that they should be instantly sterilised and the men castrated. It is pointless suggesting that the mother wouldn't know, the first person the little child would cry to, would be the mother. Neither parent should be allowed to bring any more children into the world. I know that there are lots of 'do-gooders' who will excuse *anything.* That is why we have been able to sweep this ghastly crime, under the carpet for so long. The pleasure some people take from cruelty, can be likened to when the people watched the sadistic killings of the victims in the Amphitheatres of Rome. Many of the people were recorded to have been titillated by the horror.

I think that changes are here at last, *Thank heavens.* With the Jimmy Saville revelations, more children are being believed and more cases are coming to light. People of both sexes are at last revealing the horrors they endured as kids, often by the clergy and in care homes. Where ever a man is able to get his hands on a youngster of either sex, in complete privacy—there is a need to monitor. Even music teachers, who have children to their homes alone, have been found to be untrustworthy. Not all obviously, but they should be checked very thoroughly.

I hope that all paedophiles are shaking in their boots, soon the truth will be told and age is no protector. I also hope that suitable punishment is handed out, no paltry fines. After all, the victim is destroyed for life.

Knowing how often I was menaced by spooky blokes as a young girl, I made certain that my daughter was never out at night alone. It was worrying enough in the daytime, having to endure the knowledge that perverts existed. Even then, she did have a close encounter on the way to school. It was in the morning when you would imagine things would be a degree safer for kids.

She was stopped by a man who wanted to take her into the bushes. After being interviewed by the Dulwich police who came to the school, it was regarded as serious and eventually he was caught. The police said that her description of him, given first to the teacher and then to them, enabled them to get him. I am terribly glad that my daughter and I have always managed to sidestep the dangers that befell us; she has a girl of her own now. I pray that she will be safe, she is young and beautiful. Like us, I hope that she will always get away with close encounters of the sexual kind.

Lately, I have been wondering actually *why* so many men desire little children? Maybe it is the innocence of the child, they like to impose their will on them and enjoy the resultant shock. Often forceful sex pleases men.

How did early man treat women and children? We know the human ancients, used to eat flesh, small butchered bones have been found deep in caves. They were children's bones. Maybe children were used as sex objects too? It doesn't bear thinking about does it.

This is my possible theory. Maybe *early man,* who had the original animal 'urge', felt that he had to take by force. It is just that it isn't acceptable in modern times. Maybe males subjugate the urge subconsciously, even without knowing that they do. Maybe some slip back to some primal behaviour. *It was pretty common in Victorian times.* Little girls were kept in Brothels and sold to men, some girls were very young. I have noticed that when successful men get to a certain age, they are likely to have experienced most things 'experience-able', they hanker for the unusual as their palates are often jaded. This is when they are tempted to go for the very young. It is similar to a person who has eaten all the delicacies in life and hungers for the more unusual. This is my theory; I am not trained to understand the human condition. Life is dangerous.

I can now imagine any males reading these words, being deeply outraged, this is inevitable but unnecessary.

Most guys are caring and protective of women and the young. I am speaking of those who are not. I love men and have had many happy experiences in my lifetime and now I am very senior. However, I have had more than my fair share of dangerous moments and am resourceful enough to avoid the disasters that could have occurred. If only there was a way to teach the young what is out there, without frightening them stiff. Making them afraid to go out and have fun.

Life is fragile though and my luck held. No matter how clued up we are, luck plays a large hand in protecting our children.

It is amazing how my instincts often warned me as a child. Trouble is, sometimes they did not. The guy, who tried to molest me in the country lane, had previously helped me to catch Shandy, when he wouldn't come to be haltered. He lent over his garden fence with a bowl of corn enticing him, grabbing his forelock whilst I ran up with the halter. As I profusely thanked him, I didn't get any 'vibes' warning me that he was dangerous.

Chapter Fourteen

As I matured, I longed for life with excitement of the right kind. My sister offered to let me share a flat with her in South London as she had a husband who studied all the time becoming a Civil Engineer, they also had a little baby. I could babysit and she could then have some kind of a life. The flat was a bit depressing. They rented it and it had no bath. It had an outside loo, but we made the best of it. It was a bit hilarious when there was a fog as the fog would swirl in to the loo under the door and when you were in *repose*, sitting in the fog was quite an experience. There were nice public baths in Goose Green, an area not too far from where we lived. These were proper hot baths, not just swimming baths. They were kept spotless. We went only twice a week in those days. We did not have a shower, but we used to 'strip wash'. We didn't really think we were deprived, we were just glad of a home. Accommodation in London so close to the city, was expensive, even then. We did find that we tended to get grubby though, the coal fires made the London air dirty and our clothes, particularly the collars, were in need of a wash after one wearing. Heaven knows what gunge went into the lungs of the smokers, both my sister and her husband smoked. I couldn't afford to, but I wouldn't have even if I was affluent.

I got a job near St. Pauls' Cathedral. Kings and Queens for centuries had donned their robes in my building before entering the cathedral. It was subsequently called Wardrobe Chambers and fascinated me because of its age.

The Dickensian looking offices had sloping floors. The stairs were narrow and steep. It was built in a square of ancient buildings.

We had an old lamplighter man who came into the little square at dusk and lit up the gas lamps before dark. It was so very quaint. Hitler managed to miss it, nothing was knocked down. When evening mists descended, I felt as though I was in an old fashioned novel.

Before Christmas, St. Paul's choristers sang carols and they were played through speakers outside the cathedral. I would stand in awe listening, a country girl, surrounded by this wonderful atmosphere. When there were 'Pea Souper' fogs, meaning very thick ones—(*often in winter in those days, because everyone burned coal*), it looked spooky outside my office window, with the gleam of the orangey lamplight shining through the mist—I expected Jack the Ripper any minute.

I remember a terrible night when I was returning from night school at Catford, South London. There was very thick 'pea soup' fog and a train crashed at Hither Green. Just along the line from Catford. It rolled down the bank and many people were killed. It was not long before Christmas, fortunately I was returning to our flat by bus and not train. It was a terrible thing and I thanked my lucky stars that I would be having a Christmas . . . unlike so many.

I went to London to find a broader existence. There were coffee houses, Jazz clubs, night clubs and Carnaby Street. I went to a couple of Jazz clubs. Trouble was I felt terribly claustrophobic down in the cellars. Girls fainted and were carried out over men's heads. The music was exciting of course and many names that were to become famous later in a big way, played. No, I preferred ice skating at Queens with friends, or going to the odd party. I never tried strange looking drinks or cigarettes . . . Mother had warned me. Although they *do* say, if you can remember the sixties, you weren't there. *I was*, but I can certainly remember most of it.

However, in other ways, London had so much to see. I ended up revelling in the history and the age of the city. I read all about Jack the Ripper and visited all the grisly spots . . . I had a thoroughly wonderful time there, exploring. It was a good 'growing up' experience and there were old warehouses that were backing onto the river and old pubs to drink in, my eyes stood out like chapel hat pegs. Of course, these areas are terribly 'Trendy' now with flats and houses worth a *fortune*. I used to go running in this area some years later and could see the new developments happening fast.

Chapter Fifteen

Before going back to London, my work in Malvern had been at Schweppes, strangely enough, my sister had worked there ten years before me. The company was situated in Colwall, just over the hills from Malvern. I loved the products of this company, Bitter Lemon and the Tonic Water—yum. It was the ideal spot to site it, with a ready supply of natural sparkling spring water. The springs were right there and all ready for the use of. I felt that no company could have been situated in more beauty, the setting was lovely.

I worked in the office and learned shorthand, taught to me in my spare time, by the director's secretary, a sweet little lady of advanced years. We had the factory at the back of the premises. It made the flavourings and jams for 'Roses' products amongst other things. Roses were also part of Schweppes. Wasps would fly in for a look around all the time. I was glad that striped things that flew caused me no fear. I used to collect bees as a small child. I would put my hand over the top of the jam jar to keep them in. They never stung. I suppose they knew a child had got them. Bees are said to be clever. Things generally only sting as a defence and if you keep calm they will inspect, NOT INJECT. Some of my colleagues used to bat the wasps and then they would get mad. I used to show them how I would let the little critters crawl over my arm and by holding still they would soon see that there wasn't any sugar there and fly away.

The only glitch to the job was my immediate boss— she was a natural bully. Being un-married and not going out with anyone, I think she was a frustrated person. She was not in the first flush of youth and she was single. She hadn't had a lot of luck with men. She was catty and nasty to me and made my life hell. It put me off women in charge. Maybe someone superior to her should have dealt with her, she was doubtless jealous of me because I was young and attractive. I realise now that she was an object for pity. Then, I suffered and cried at home and hated going to work.

This was the time when the Cuban missile crisis was occurring. I was so obsessed with my miserable existence at work that it all passed me by rather, maybe it was a good thing in retrospect. The general feeling then, was of fear. The world came near to a disaster. Thankfully, we all came through it and I even survived my hateful boss.

I used to travel on the train with two old brothers who worked at Colwall, growing roses at the nurseries. They lived in a cottage alongside the river Severn. They told me many tales of life on the riverbank. They were unique countrymen; few would exist today like them. They drew water from their pump outside and loved their rustic life. Neither married though—they had looked after the old folk. Now **they** were the old folk, I wonder who looked after *them*. Of course as a friend pointed out to me; nowadays, two elderly gentlemen saving a seat for a young woman on a train, would cause eyebrows to raise . . . isn't it sad, it is all so different now. It was a much simpler time then, yet it WAS dangerous as previous chapters have outlined. These two dear old chaps never uttered a word out of place though and taught me much country lore.

I also met and chatted to Dame Laura Knight, the wonderful artist who specialised in ancient Gypsy Caravan, log fire type scenes and ballet dancers. She was famous and I think, lived in Colwall at that time. She was a member of the Royal Academy and a top selling artist. She isn't in vogue now, even though her work is very charming. It is all abstract or impressionist art that seems to go with modern decor, which people want.

I still love the beauty of the painted animal though, especially the horse. I personally love to paint, animals and horses especially. I paint flowers in watercolour too. It is so relaxing and I love the fine detail—no impressions for me. It is a great hobby. It is amazing how many people can create a spectacular picture if they try. If you can't paint, try writing. It is great to give your kids a 'first hand' record of events to read and one day pass on to their children, about how Granny lived and the times. It is also very cathartic to get it all down, I am surprised how much I can remember, good and bad. One item of memory seems to jog another, they say that as we get older, we remember things further back and it is true.

Many families seemed to disintegrate after the1960's, now they often leave old people to go it alone. The old folk often end up seeing no member of the family, year in, year out.

This country should revise its way of treating the older person and they in turn, should become less self-centred and give more affection and physical love to their children when they are small. There is neglect in Care homes and Hospital wards. We are good at giving to charity in this country, but hopeless at respecting our own aging population. Too many individuals are selfish, many mothers never tell their children that they love them, or kiss them enough. Too many do not read to them or play with them.

I don't want to fall in to the trap of comparing everything from the past, with happenings now. These comparisons often don't stack up because such events are subject to modernisation. Things are bound to differ and many to the good, especially the way that children and older people are starting to read with the e-readers much more. Books are coming back in, thank heavens.

There is one thing however, that certainly hasn't improved and that is the attitude of some parents to their children. I still see a huge gulf between parent and child. This is a problem of all classes. We know that in the past, the wealthy used to bung their kids into boarding school. Sometimes, they were far too young. That got them out of the way conveniently, whilst Mummy and Daddy pursued the lifestyle that was best not disturbed by their children. This is done less and less today and there is the computer to keep in visual touch when families *have* to be parted. Kids are sent away from home at later ages now. I hope this will stop the 'separation' damage that was regularly caused. Many people who went to boarding schools will say 'It never hurt me' but how would they know? As we all know, there are some who should have their children removed permanently in this world, sadists will always be out there unfortunately.

Within the group of parents who refuse to work and haven't for generations, there are those who have many kids to get larger houses from their housing departments—they don't really want children, basically, they are spongers. Although they find that they are hampered by the children, the older ones bring up the younger ones. They prefer to breed as more money comes in to fund their households. To them, anything is better than working. Other than that scenario, there are parents who simply don't seem glad to own their children. There is little kissing and hugging and telling them that they are loved. If this continues, the child when adult will be hopeless at showing feelings—not only to their wives and kids, but to the older generation as well. No wonder there is considerable abandonment of the elderly. Some grown children hardly ever bother to visit them, on hospital wards or in their homes. This could be remedied if we all 'loved' more. To love, you have to have *been* loved—it is a learnt emotion when young.

I often see Mothers looking totally disinterested, when walking down the road to the shopping centre, with their kids in pushchairs. I frequently see them as they pass my house. They are texting as they walk and their children are facing away from them in their chairs, there is no connection between mother and child. Who designed the pushchairs to face that way? What must a young baby feel when about to cross the road and is turned towards the kerb to cross, the lorry wheels looming above them and no mother between them and the traffic? It must be terrifying and *they* can't speak.

These poor children will probably become Grandparents one day who are pretty indifferent to *their* Grandchildren. Away facing chairs lessen the bond between parent and child and are dangerous as well, you would never know if anything was wrong with the little one as you just couldn't see them. My push chair faced towards me and my children used to smile at me and I would talk to them all the time. We are very close now—maybe that is why. Why have children if you do not really want them? There is the 48 hour pill if you think that you have conceived. It may cause a bit of a headache but unwanted kids cause headaches for years.

Chapter Sixteen

I must return to events in my younger life. Later, after the interlude in London, I returned to Malvern and worked at the Ministry of Defence. It was secret work, mainly to do with Radar maintenance. I signed the official secrets act and was sworn not to talk. I didn't want to talk—I wanted LIFE and fun—all that heavy stuff at such a young age, it was tedious and the people I worked with weren't young enough and most were dotty as they were scientists.

There were many funny tales told on the grapevine about scientists parking in London for meetings and then coming home on the train, forgetting that they had taken the car. One, used to walk around with a basket on his *head, wearing pink tights.* You see these guys were just too brilliant for their own good. I wanted ordinary fun loving people around me and when I returned to London, that is what I got.

I had spent most of my earnings on clothes being a young girl and the cost of travel in London seemed to have increased a lot. I was too young to have saved for a car of my own. I did not have much money left, after giving my sister and her husband money for keep. I had enough for a few pretty dresses though. The fashion was very feminine then, hooped underskirts to make the circular 'Cut on the cross' skirts, stand out and wide belts that made the waist look small.

A lot of us tried to look like Doris Day, in her wonderful films of the time. The shoes were a bit pointed, but light not clumpy and the heels high. I looked taller then and having a 24 inch waist, made the outfits very fetching. I wore my long dark hair up in a French pleat, and I felt very 'noticeable' in my little red 'monkey' jacket with the full skirt billowing out below the nipped in waist.

I got a lot of compliments and in those days, wolf whistles were not politically incorrect. I was always grateful, even if it was someone from a building site . . . How bad is it to recognise a good looking girl and let her know? Everyone would have a day that was just a little bit better.

We all seem afraid of doing or saying, the wrong thing now. Perhaps some women were not so self assured as me. Maybe some poor girls could find wolf whistles pretty scary.

However, life is so much more serious now with jobs hard to find, I really worry about the future. I would be hard put to find a wolf whistler on a building site now, sites are rare and the workers who *are* employed are nose to the grindstone, working long hours and hard at it. Most of the building sites around Kent and London seem to be staffed by eastern European guys anyway. They work hard for less and are nice people, for them it is head down for a full day of slogging; they have to send lots of cash home to mamma I expect. They have suffered and starved as nations that were overrun by the Germans in the war, it sure ensures the work ethic, if it is obtainable, go for it. We haven't starved and been cruelly treated, it makes such a difference.

The young will not even realise how many jobs have been and are being lost, thanks to computers and technology in general. I realise that jobs were created by technology as well, but it took several men to carry out the functions that one computer could do and much better. Certainly, it was the banks that hold responsibility for this current dreadful recession. Many names that we have grown up with have gone forever. What will the future hold for people? Back then, in the sixties, life was less complex, free love and breaking the stranglehold of parental control was mainly what teenagers wanted. We couldn't have imagined what was to come in the future; we were all having such new freedom and loving it.

Teddy Boys, Mod's and Rockers, whatever was your thing. Style counted, now it is piercings, 'Grunge' and Tattoos. It is not a good time for fashion. It could be that I am just too 'old fashioned' however . . . all this covering up of the legs with leggings, the girls do not even wear skirts over the top and we see all sorts of shapes and sizes which would look much more elegant, tastefully draped in a cute skirt. Tight jeans always look nice but those leggings are awful and don't even let the sun reach places where it is needed for the vitamin D *and in the summer too.* We should bare as much as possible to the sun, as we do not get too much of it. Just be tasteful, bellies and bosoms should not hang out. There are men here from countries' which assume women are no good, if they show everything. It is useless saying that they shouldn't think that way—*they do.* There is enough danger, around us. In this country, women reveal their hair and their legs. Both are naturally beautiful and should be revealed. I am not worried about that, but coming home from the nightclubs in the taxi's, driven by men from some countries who are not liberated, or educated—is very dodgy *when wearing hardly any clothes.* I have witnessed girls coming out in the early hours of the morning, to pick up their cabs in drastically revealing stuff and they have often had one to many too. During my life in London at a certain point, I was mini-cabbing. I had to sometimes do the late shift. That meant collecting these young girls and taking them home. I mainly picked up the females as I was a lady driver. At least they were safe with me. However I'm afraid I soon gave that up. It just took one of them to be sick in my car and that was an end to it. It didn't take me long to give the *whole* idea up—there were men who dealt drugs in the back of the motor. I may have received large tips when this happened, but it was not the occupation for a woman. All this took place after my Mum passed away and I had the use of my evenings and nights. I was also based in South London which was an unsuitable place to be a woman alone in a car and picking up strange guys at night.

However, to get back to what I was saying about fashion and when I was a girl.

When I was young in the sixties, our shoes had points. The points often didn't lay flat because they were empty, unless you had a long big toe. Girls often crammed their toes into the pointy bit at the front. Consequently, bunions were often formed. This painful condition is where the bone becomes deformed at the outside of the big toe, right where the toes join the foot. I was lucky to have short square feet, size two and a half. My toes wouldn't be able to get crammed in the point, they just wouldn't go. Although I am ancient, I have perfect feet and get praised when I go for a pedicure. All feet should have room to spread naturally. The shoe designers know this, they just don't care. They just create new styles to make the existing shoes have to be replaced. That is what fashion is about, *money*. It is o.k. I guess, but cruel if it causes deformities. If your future job is fixing ancient feet,

Podiatrists will at least have loads of work. Corns and other foot problems could be avoided so easily though, it is a shame.

When I was a mother-to-be, we women were proud of being pregnant too, but we liked to wear things to cover the bump in a pretty way. No stretched T—shirts for us that revealed an area of pregnant belly. Why do girls think that looks cute? To me, it is distasteful and common looking. I used to wear dungarees, long shirts over jeans or pregnancy dresses. I looked sweet when I was pregnant and was proud of looking pregnant. Men used to stand up to offer a seat on the buses and trains. I understand they don't these days. How badly mannered they must be. I could not have worked up to eight and a half months if I couldn't have got a seat, the journey was quite long. Have manners vanished now? I sure hope not, manners show respect and you can't have too much of that in life. After the war, money was short in general. Catalogue clothes kept even the worst off looking good. It was the 1960's and my things came from a catalogue, but I constantly received nice things said, from both men and women. The point of buying from the catalogue was that although some things were a little more expensive than on the High street, one had time to pay. It was useful. Now purchase is on-line usually, I am told. Girls are so busy trying to make ends meet. The convenience of time saving by on-line shopping is inevitable. However, in my youth, I had a good figure and just enough money to adorn it well and have fun.

"Flower Power" was in full swing but I didn't party much, I was too busy trying to better myself with night school. I was also expected to mind my nephew, for his Mummy and Daddy when they were out. However, you could bet your life that as soon as they disappeared to the cinema or wherever, that little nephew of mine would fill his nappy and squawk—I had to do the honours, it is a wonder that I ended up with three of my own after that.

I soon had fun in another way however. I had met my first real boyfriend and we used to babysit together. If my dear sister Daphne had known what her sister got up to snogging, she'd have had a fit. But we knew how to make the most of our time with very little cash. One has to grow up after all.

We did see the odd show however, 'The Pyjama Game' was a great favourite with Ted Hockridge and Elizabeth Seal, it was magic and the songs were great. That was my very first 'Grown Up' theatrical visit. Of course there were pantomimes when I was little. I was even *in one* with Fred Wilby as producer. I got paid. I was one of the 'Starlight Babes' and I could dance, both ballet and tap, also sing. It was great fun, hard work, but fun. He even wanted me for one of the babes in 'Babes in the wood' his next production but Mum wouldn't let me go, sad—I might have had a different career in showbiz.

The joy of going to the very first adult musical is something to remember though.

However, the boyfriend and I didn't need drugs or alcohol, love was the drug and it cost nothing. They were the best days, becoming an adult and breaking the umbilical—poor Mother, all on her own in Malvern, but it is natural to be selfish when you are just a girl.

All too soon, my boyfriend had to go off and do his National Service, it having been deferred for him to take his articles in accountancy. I was devastated and moved back to be with Mother who was lonely and sad as well. She missed us too much. I had to go home.

Chapter Seventeen

Time passed and I met the man who was to become my husband. What an error of judgment, a folly . . . this story takes a darker turn from now on.

It was at a party that I first saw him, he was playing 'Liar Dice' it was a form of Poker, but with dice instead of cards. He was a deadly player—I stood and watched him, you couldn't read his face. He beat all the other players and with his crooked little smile I was infatuated immediately. The attraction was mutual, so we became an 'item.' He looked a bit like Charlton Heston, a tall blond, strong, hunky type and in his uniform (he was a Flying Officer in the RAF) my head was turned.

Of course the fact that he was a brilliant cool liar didn't seem to warn me about him—I just would have *drunk his bath water* I was so infatuated. We both worked at the same establishment, he was stationed there, being a pretty clever young man. Soon Mum was keeping a watchful eye on me—she didn't like him. She said he was too much like her ex. husband, *the worst thing she could have said*, I was drawn even closer then. All Mums should know that kids usually flout their opinions.

I thought he was mysterious and wonderful, it was love I'm afraid and we hatched our wedding plans. We married in the autumn. I wore red. I always said that if it was a spring wedding, I would be in white with red flowers or if in the winter, red with white flowers. The scarlet woollen sheath dress looked fabulous with the white bouquet and my jaunty little straw boater with the red ribbons just finished the ensemble off. The wedding was in a Registry Office. It was a very pretty wedding and a very pretty venue.

Malvern is such a lovely place for photographs. The office is in a gorgeous park with the hills as a backdrop. It was an inexpensive wedding because my mother couldn't manage more, but all his other Officer colleagues came and formed up as we came out. It was thrilling. I didn't need grandeur. I had my dream husband, Gordon. Well, I certainly believed it at the time. Only his mother turned up for our big day, the rest of his family 'blanked us.' I was to find out that he had been engaged to a girl who was an artist, her father was a Wing Commander, he broke it off when he met me, her family if they had known the sort of husband he was to become, would have been glad. Gordon's family must have thought that this marriage to the other girl would have had him promoted to dizzy heights in the R.A.F. A little thing like *love* didn't worry them. They were not very nice people I was to find out, I wasn't sad that they didn't come, we had very little money, feeding them would have cost the earth.

His family liked me even less when I talked him out of the RAF. I didn't want to be a service wife. Mum's husband was also an officer in the services and it didn't do her much good. I also felt that I wasn't conventional enough. I would say wrong stuff. With my upbringing, I always called a 'spade a spade' and probably wasn't too tactful. I was brought up to be a free spirit, galloping around on a horse and not giving a damn for anyone's opinions, how could I suddenly become quiet about my views and be conventional as well? Shopping and other feminine pursuits, I did because I had to, but only when necessary. Shopping was never a therapy to me, and still isn't . . . it is a bore. I would sooner read a good book than slog around Marks and Sparks or somewhere. I make my clothes last and last as I am not prone to fashion worries.

Maybe half the reason for my disinterest in how I looked for most of my life was because I had grown up tree climbing with a gang of lads, never being out of jeans or jodhpurs. We were such tomboys, we three girls who were in the gang. Jeans and shorts were the uniform.

We got up to dangerous things, but no adult knew. We had a 'gang house' in a wood where we cooked stolen bits of food over a fire we built, it was child heaven. We didn't drink, we were innocent kids. The worst thing was the odd stolen Woodbine cigarette. There was no violence or gang 'culture', such things were not known about in Malvern, or in fact, those days. Probably the film 'West Side Story' was the first time I was conscious of gang fights. It all seemed terribly American to me. It was to be a few years before 'Mod's and Rockers' fought at the seaside on the beaches.

Yes, we kids were pretty innocuous. A couple of times I remember—someone brought a bottle of cider. We all had a swig and acted drunk—we felt drunk. It was all in the mind in those days. Such games as tracking in the ferns were our amusement.

To give an example of our immaturity, once when one of the boys called Frank, had begun to grow up. He rashly said 'Kiss', when we were playing 'Truth, dare, kiss or promise'. I had to give him my scarf as a forfeit, as I had refused to kiss him—we all took a dim view of that. We never used 'kiss'—so we removed him out of the gang.

Poor Frank was never seen again, he was just too mature for us.

Life in the country is great for children. I feel sad for the townies. My older cousin visiting from London thought when he saw sprouts growing in the garden, that they were little trees.

I wasn't evacuated in the war because I was born in the country. For many children it was the best experience possible, despite missing their parents.

Chapter Eighteen

As soon as Gordon left the RAF, we both moved to Dulwich. He worked in a company that was concerned with Corrosion Engineering or 'Cathodic' Protection, a new field in engineering. Basically in layman's terms, it was using cathodes to attract corrosion (rust) to sacrificial metals, so that the undersea legs of oil platforms or big oil tanks or even pipes, wouldn't corrode with rust. He went away often. He went to Libya and met Colonel Gaddafi. He told me that his eyes were crazy looking and glittering. I was impressed.

When I discovered condoms in his packing once, he told me they were for protecting the Cathodes. I can't think how he fooled me, I believed it . . . they were going under water weren't they and didn't need protecting. How he must have laughed behind my back.

I did have one suspicious time however, when I actually noticed something. We went to the 'Talk of the Town' when we were honeymooning. It was in the West End. A beautiful showgirl danced the whole time looking at him. We had a table at the front of stage and he gave her one of his crooked little smiles and they wiggled eyebrows and did a good job of flirting with each other, the whole show. It spoilt it for me. Gordon said that I was being stupid, but a woman knows when something torrid is taking place and it was the shape of things to come.

Ages after that incident, he bought me perfume called 'Rive Gauche', he asked me to wear it. I was so thrilled that he had bought me perfume. I found out later that he was having an affair with one of the secretaries and she wore it. If I detected her perfume on him, he would have a built in excuse. No wonder he was so brilliant at Poker, he could lie for England.

I didn't get totally disillusioned until after we had had our two darling babies. Although once when I held his hand in front of his parents, he said to me 'we don't do that here'—dropping my hand like a hot potato. I was shocked, I didn't know about narrow mindedness. I would have been proud to hold my hand if I were him and we were married at the time.

Oh well, I was young and despite all, later on I thought we had the perfect marriage and the perfect family, one boy and one girl. They were good babies, contented and happy, but he didn't have any interest in being a family man at all. We shouldn't have got married in the first place, we were too young and only infatuated with each other—we mistook it for love. It is easy to be wise after the event they say, and it's true.

He was very unkind though. He gave me no money and wouldn't let me drive the company car. I was deprived of love and never taken on holiday. It was all just *'cooking and babies'*. There were no compliments and no praise. I was a dog's body. He wouldn't even make love, and after many cruelties and not just mental ones either, I took my doctor's advice and got a job. I had found out at the firm's annual Christmas Dinner, that the other wives could all drive the company's cars. I soon insisted in doing the same.

I got a job. I became a jewellery seller—party plan, nice stuff with a guarantee and good design. It was evenings, so fitted in with having a family. I was good at selling. The commission gave me freedom and I recruited the friends that I had made. That put me at a higher level (I guess it was a form of Pyramid selling). The product was super though and sold like hot cakes. I eventually became a manager, quite elevated with a salary as well as commission. Gordon wasn't proud, he was angry that my earnings were considerable. He made my life as difficult as possible, as I had to go out some evenings. Somehow I managed and climbed the ranks.

I loved the girls who worked under me. There was a particularly sweet one named Stephanie, who later on helped me in my personal life.

Those days were such fun, but I clipped Gordon's wings because I was out in the car. One evening the event was cancelled and I arrived home early, there he was in a compromising position, *bonking*, in my breakfast room. The female, was one who I had tried to recruit to do the job with me. No wonder she petered out and was no good, all she really wanted was to come in to my house as soon as I left for work.

I was mortified and embarrassed. He said he was sorry and promised to be good from then on—he begged me to believe him. I must have needed a psychiatrist . . . no one should be that green. I really did believe him though. I *thought that he would value his marriage and children* more than losing it by cheating. What an idiot I was, he couldn't resist that girl and he used to find ways of meeting her behind my back. She was married too, oh dear her poor unsuspecting husband. I flirted with the idea of letting him know. He had health problems though and was having facial surgery at the time. I felt that he should not have that bombshell as soon as he returned home. I expect he found out eventually that his wife was a lying cheat, they didn't have children, so I hope he dumped her. Why do these women who like married men, choose the ones with children?

My husband had me well worked out. He knew that my heart was soft and that I had no money saved. He made sure of it, because as soon as I was earning, he gave me none at all. He made me pay for everything. I couldn't save. It certainly worked.

He saved secretly.

He bought gold, rand and sovereigns. I saw them one day when he left the drawer at the base of our large wardrobe in the bedroom, open—for a moment. I was such a busy mother working, dealing with the home and the children, I foolishly let things go. I should have queried how much money was there. I guess I assumed he was saving for our family. I just can't believe that my curiosity wasn't aroused. I suppose that I thought that men kept a private space and we didn't have a desk with a lock. I think he put them in a bank for safe keeping once I had seen them, there were lots. He could have saved a fortune with my working and doing so well. He must have known that we would not stay together, he was preparing for his future.

Chapter Nineteen

It was around this time that my Grandmother and her husband had the mother of all rows. She left him to come up to my house in Dulwich, for a break.

Grandma was over seventy years old at that time. Her husband being twenty years younger had found another woman and was having an affair on the sly and Grandma found out.

Oh goodness, it was shocking, the things that she vowed to do. I realised how much she loved him, she was just mortally hurt, and *I knew something about how that felt*. Gradually I talked them both round. I phoned him and told him that she was crying all the time. He came up to London to sweet talk her back to him. It seemed to work with my marriage counselling.

Whilst they were with me, I remember Gordon attacking me violently with a punch aimed at my face. Goodness knows what had upset him. He must have hated me intensely. I was the last to realize this. I just thought that he was bad tempered. I had had a lot of experience of bad tempers, living with both my mother and grandmother. I ducked and he landed the blow on my step Grandfather's shoulder. The bruise was eventually the size of a dinner plate.

I escaped into the garden just as the man from whom I had purchased a second hand car, came around with the log book. He wanted to come in and 'sort' him out. I said no, but he came back on the Monday to find out if I needed any help.

My Grandparents had lent me a bit of money to buy an old car thankfully. His name was Guy and he took me down to the local pub and bought me lunch. He was kind, and full of advice about my leaving this man. He said that no husband should hit a woman, especially one who was six feet two. I was only five foot one. The contest was in no way equal. He had the power to really damage me. I had an ally, things would look up now.

The car purchase was in the summertime.

I decided to chance a holiday with the children and all the relatives. It was lovely weather and a visit to Cornwall seemed like a great idea. My new car would carry us, but my husband insisted in coming as well. I was paying for the chalet hire. We had to use his car, to accommodate us all. It was larger inside and it turned out to be a good thing later. As I was paying for everything, food included, he wanted to come. He was squeaky mean, if only I had said NO.

The children needed a break and so did I. Mother and my Grandparents came from Malvern, with Mother driving them. The car they came in was Grandma's. Even my Sister and family came with us, from Surrey, where they had moved. It should have been the finest holiday ever—all my loved ones together, at the same time.

When we arrived, the one *fly in the ointment*, Gordon, was unhappy. I expect he missed whichever female he was seeing.

One night he threw me out of bed because he said that I had too many bed clothes and he had none. I was asleep and woke up with a start, to find myself on the floor. I was shocked and ran 'Home to Mum'. Mum was in the chalet next door. That was the only time that I could run to Mum when I experienced cruelty. She was sharing with my Grandparents. Daphne and family were in the chalet, next to them and in blissful ignorance of the shenanigans next door.

Although it was dreadful for me with a person who despised me, and patently obviously didn't want to be there, I put up with it and for the sake of everyone, the row passed.

How silly was I? To have let him come with us in the first place . . . Mum could have shared with the children and me. It could have been much more fun, with loads of games to amuse us when it rained or when we wanted to be in.

Sadly it *did* rain. The North coast of Cornwall isn't the driest place. The claustrophobic nature of the small chalets began to take a toll. Soon an even more dreadful event happened.

Mum once again rubbed her mother and stepfather up the wrong way. There was a really bad row over something, culminating in Mother telling them that she would not drive them home.

They had provoked her and been wicked. At last Mum had a way to get revenge. Without further ado, the Grandparents phoned for a cousin to come down from Malvern on the train and drive them back.

How bad the row was I didn't witness; I was in my own hell next door and it rained and rained making things worse.

I was shattered and took Mum back to Dulwich with us. At least Gordon's company car was spacious.

Whilst Mother was recovering and I was comforting her in Dulwich. Her belongings from where she had been living at Grandma's were put out in bags. My old saddles and bridles and other equine stuff that Mum had looked after for me, were just given away, along with all of my childhood possessions. I expect it was to my cousin. I didn't know for sure, but he never spoke to me again which I took as a sign of guilt. Up to then, he had been reasonably friendly whenever I met him.

Mum returned to Malvern to no home and no belongings, and my last connection to childhood was lost forever. This was also the last eviction by my Grandmother . . . she had her final revenge too.

Mum had to go and stay in a hostel. She had made herself homeless by letting the prefab go and returning to look after her mother, when Grandma and her husband had split up.

Previously, before Mother and Grandmother, split up forever. When Mum was still in her Mother's life, Grandma had a dreadful accident. She scalded herself when she fainted. She was making tea, and fell forward onto the area where the electric kettle was plugged in. They didn't have 'cut-outs' in those days, instead most kettles would work by the section on the lead, that one pushed into the kettle, shooting out when it boiled dry. She could have been killed—but she fell to the floor before the scalding became lethal.

Her wound was shocking, but incredibly she survived. When Mother went round at lunch time to make her a meal, she found Grandma on the floor and got the ambulance. They dressed her head in hospital and Mother played nurse in the ensuing weeks. I expect that was the one time that she was able to get close to her. Her husband was still in terrible disgrace from his affair and the two of them weren't speaking, despite the injury to his wife's head.

Mother was encouraged by Grandma to give up her home, which was expensive to run on one income. She moved down to her mothers' again, occupying the little flat that was in the house from when Grandma's third daughter and husband had lived there.

That is how she became homeless, when she was turned out. I never dreamed that by healing the rift between the Grandparents, my own Mother would be thrown out and her belongings destroyed and mine lost. It was so sad that Grandma was a viscous and sadistic woman and had always been so. *Leopards do not change their spots.* Imagine how my Mother must have suffered when the council pulled down the prefabs and re-housed the occupants in purpose built bungalows. She would have been secure for life.

She endured the loss of a wonderful opportunity. I was so angry that I wrote a searing letter to my Grandmother telling her that she had been wicked and cruel. I had been told she was, and now that I was an adult, I saw it for myself. I suggested that as she was old and always banging on about how bad folk always got their *'come uppance,'* she should be afraid of what was waiting for her. She promptly disinherited me and never spoke my name again. I didn't mind, *she wasn't fit to speak my name.* She had destroyed my mother. Imagine getting almost to retirement age and having to live in a hostel. It made Mother very vulnerable.

Chapter Twenty

I do sometimes feel sorry for myself. I would have loved a nice grandmother, one who loved me and who I can have nice memories of. I lost my entire family—all my relatives except one. Cousin Gillian. I knew her as Jilly, but alas I hardly ever saw her. She only had half a lung left. She was a poor little thing who permanently hovered between life and death. She managed to grow up though and she married. I'm told it amazed everyone. She later had a son, strong and good looking. She lived on a bushel of pills. I think that she took antibiotics permanently. There was an ever present worry of chest infection, poor soul. Fragile people so regularly, seem to have a gentle and sweet nature. Poor little Jilly *had*, I never heard her say a bad word about anyone.

I once invited her to my house in London, with her husband. Her son was in the forces at the time. She loved her stay and loved me. She used to talk about me to others and always referred to me as 'Our Ann'. It meant so much to me. She was a family member who didn't reject us cruelly. Her father and my mother were sister and brother, most of the family shunned my mother but I should have liked some relatives. I know it sounds childish and pathetic—but I longed for a big loving family, one who I could sometimes gossip about and make phone calls to. No one wanted to know us and no one wanted to know Jilly really, she looked frail and was a bit slow. No wonder she loved coming up to our house in London. She would have felt very sophisticated. I wish I had been able to know her for longer. She passed away when she was far too young.

I am pretty sure that Grandmother disparaged my mother, to all who would listen. As she was pretty affluent, most of the family, if they sucked up enough, hoped for something in the future will. Greed is a nasty thing.

My mother, my grandmother, me, and my daughter.

My beautiful granddaughter in Australia.

My grandmother driving her car with friends.

Me and my horse Shandy.

Our Wonderful Prefab

The ship my Grandfather sailed on

A photo taken by my Grandfather whilst on his travels

The Author with her favourite cat Willy Wonka

My mother put her little life savings into the purchase of a caravan which was stored temporarily at a council site in Worcester. It was big and roomy. She was on the point of retiring and it was a way out of the pickle she was in. The Council however, wrote to her and said that it was taking up space and if she didn't find a site for it immediately, they would charge her the back rent for the storage.

She simply couldn't find a site for a Residential van anywhere. Site owners only let van owners have sites, if they bought the van from them. Whoever sold Mum that van, must have known that she would be stuck without a site. How could they have been so cruel? What a fix.

I drove around Surrey trying to get someone to have her, no luck. Then when I was near to tears, a man on a Surrey site gave me a phone number of a site in Kent. He said he would speak to the site manager there and that I should phone this man the next day.

The guy understood the fix we were in and said that I should drive down to Hoo on the Isle of Grain and meet him. He was very kind but I felt that he had 'expectations' of a reward. He was a little too friendly. *He was stroking my leg as we spoke.* I had to promise to go to dinner with him when my Mother was sited there. He even offered to bring the van up from Worcester to Kent on his low loader, all for a nominal fee. When I phoned Mother and told her that her troubles were over, she wept with relief.

I had to find a way to get out of the situation with the site manager, not until she was safe though. Anyhow, it all went well. A pretty site was found for her, and one could hear the little jingly sounds of the mast bells on the yachts moored there. It was a Marina and spectacular, she was overjoyed.

We painted and papered and dug and planted. It was such a beautiful place, and the site manager was so nice to her. I pulled a fast one, I said that my partner was so thrilled with his kindness that he wanted to come and meet him with a bottle of single malt and thank him personally. He said that wasn't necessary and accepted the bottle from me instead. I had pulled it off, my devious plan. When he realised that I had a boyfriend, he had a re-think. There wasn't a need for any other form of reward—apart from the undying gratitude of my mother. He wasn't a risk to older women, thank goodness, he preferred them young. I had a narrow escape. I have heard of helping mother, *but that was ridiculous.*

Sadly, the lecherous Manager got beaten up rather badly, by a man whose wife he had been found with. *It really was so sad* that he had enough goodness in his heart to rescue us, yet couldn't keep his hands off others men's wives. Be sure your sins will find you out. That was what Grandma was always quoting, it could just be true.

So I had my Mother out of Malvern at last; out of her Mother's clutches and near to me so that I could visit frequently.

We chose to forget the pain of past relations, just keeping a friendship with my Aunty, her older sister. They travelled to lots of places together like Scotland and Ireland and the two of them stayed with me sometimes, in London.

They enjoyed a lovely relationship until my poor Auntie died from a heart attack. It was just as she had won the 'House' at the local Bingo hall in Worcester. It was tragic. Confucius tells us 'It is better to travel, than to arrive.' In poor Aunties case, it certainly was. I hope that there is lots of Bingo in heaven for her. Mother was devastated. They should definitely keep a defibrillator on hand and someone trained to use one, at Bingo halls.

At the same sad time, Mother discovered that she had breast cancer. Possibly all the stress brought it on, but that is another story.

When would all the pure tragedy come to an end for my poor Mother?

Gordon had turned into a monster, this wonderful handsome and elegant man. He seemed to have changed character completely. He didn't ever abuse the children though. I would have left years sooner if he had. However, the pain of seeing their Mum so unhappy could not have been good for them. He made sure that every penny that I earned, HE spent.

I was so broke and things were not so organised in those days. It was the early seventies. Leaving cruel men was almost impossible. I would have to have packed up and gone back to Malvern at the time. Mum not having yet retired.

I was too proud to tell her that she was right, he **was** bad. I tried to save situations all the time, our nerves were shot. I was offered tranquilizers but I never took them. I was scared that I would become addicted. That was when I realized that I would have to find a way to go.

Chapter Twenty One

Guy and I met a couple of times regarding car issues. We always tried to incorporate some nice happening afterwards, a walk in Dulwich Park or a game of tennis. Sometimes we just sat and gazed at the rhododendrons which were spectacular. It was such a picturesque place with an enormous lake in the middle. It was the river Effra surfacing.

That river was once big enough, that Queen Elizabeth 1st sailed up it in her barge. Like the Fleet, it was eventually piped underground. Where the pipe obviously leaked, it caused a lovely lake to exist where we would take out rowing boats. We and the kids would challenge each other to a race. Rhododendrons and azaleas bloomed in profusion; it was a truly beautiful park. We were falling in love: perhaps I should rephrase that—I WAS. He was falling in lust.

I began to look forward to seeing him enormously and before long our meetings were strictly romantic instead of strictly business. He was so attractive, not tall like my husband, only five foot ten inches, but stocky and strong with wavy blond hair and golden skin. He was sexy and I fell, hook, line and sinker. Guy was always smart; he worked in gloves to keep his nails decent. For a mechanic, he wore nice tops and jeans and there were no holes and tat. He seemed to adore my two youngsters. He was very complimentary, saying they were refined and gentle. Not a pair of battlers that were always fighting and generally not getting on.

Of course, *there was no resentment between the two children.* I had designed a three year gap between having them. The oldest had full fuss made of him without being usurped by another baby. It made life a lot easier, when the first child was not jealous of the second. When my daughter was a baby, my little lad would help me by holding her kicking legs still whilst I applied the cream or the nappy. He would sprinkle the baby powder and generally take an interest in her as a person. They have stayed close even now, time and distance makes no difference. It was 1965 when I had my second child and life was still much harder for the mother, modern devices like disposable nappies hadn't quite arrived, we soaked them in buckets of a bleach solution which stank, it kept them snowy white though. It was all very labour intensive *but everything was,* we had carpet sweepers which were put around daily and we polished. I doubt if many people bother to be so house proud nowadays. I can't blame them either. Also we were expected to have our husband's dinner ready when he arrived home from work and most men wouldn't iron or do housework in general. It is so much more relaxed nowadays. Girls still moan and groan—but it is no wonder, the poor things have to go to work and cope at home as well. Even so, both men and women tend to share the jobs, they both work so it is only fair.

In my young day, as a general rule, women stayed at home to bring their babies up. There were exceptions obviously. When people asked at dinner parties "What do you do?" It was easy to feel a bit inadequate saying that you were *just a housewife.* Eventually, we were all finding jobs to be 'stimulating' company and paying people to mind the children, you can just guess what happened. Prices started soaring, childcare started really costing the earth and someone else would see your little one take those first steps etc. So sad, women were conned. It was not long before women *had* to get jobs to make ends meet. Previously, we young wives always met up with friends and had coffee mornings in each other's houses.

Friendships would have been made when attending the various clinics. There, clever breathing techniques to assist at childbirth were taught, although they weren't much good when the event came. Drugs were the thing and natural childbirth and lofty ideals usually went out of the window. At least we all had the comfort of thinking that the pain would be controlled. It was a bit of a shock when it hurt like hell. It is amazing that we girls forget and deliberately have another child. The second one usually isn't so bad and nowadays with anaesthesia cleverly administered, I cannot imagine why women are afraid at all. A little pain is worth the final result and without my offspring; I would be lost and lonely.

After suffering further at my husband's hands and the fact that he didn't want me in the least, I felt really cheated. Why couldn't I have a decent husband like other girls? He seemed to delight in mean acts. He was also refusing to drop my children at their school drive, even though he was passing it. Seeing them running after the car because he wouldn't wait and him driving off without them, was a shockingly hurtful thing to witness. Of course, I see it all now, he was probably picking his mistress up on route and probably spending the day with her . . . I was gullible in the extreme.

He really messed up being a husband and father. He could have told me to go, I would have. I didn't lack courage. I just tried to hang on to my marriage and make it work. Mother had *said* that he wasn't the right one for me. Once, I did love him a lot, before he destroyed it. Golden rule—do not hang around where you are not wanted. Our home may have been comfortable and beautiful with its chandeliers and Persian carpets, in a lovely part of London, but there is no substitute for peace of mind.

Any man who is mentally or physically cruel, DOES NOT LOVE HIS LADY. They may say sorry and grovel afterwards, *but get out immediately*. The degree of violence will start to increase, if you stay there. He has shown you his power and you have acquiesced. There is no hope, however much you love him. There are places to go and you must not let children see horror, it damages them beyond putting right. Sometimes the children grow up to abuse their families similarly, the cycle continues. You mustn't risk this happening. They didn't ask to be born, do not make them suffer seeing their parent brutalised. The longer you stay, the worse it will be, the violent partner gets their sadistic kicks and enjoyment seeing you on the floor before them. That is why so many girls get killed, they didn't go soon enough. HE WILL NOT CHANGE. Get out and do not tell any member of his family where you are going and swear *yours* to secrecy. Blood is thicker than water. I appreciate that there are *women* who abuse their husbands also, so tragic. They do not usually murder them though; they haven't got loads of testosterone to deal with. Any abuse, *women, children, old people*—it is a terrible sin and life will punish you eventually.

Guy was working on a big ex. Lyons Bread Van. It had to go as a camper, to the South of France, for its holidaying owner. Guy mechanically fixed it and fitted it out with lockers to hold the clothes and other items. There was a shelf for lining up the mugs and plates with hooks to hang things. The left side locker held all the cooking utensils, knives and forks etc, the right one bed clothes, towels and soft things. Barring the elegance, or lack of it. It was a useful vehicle and large enough to live in. It certainly made an inexpensive camper, even without an internal window, for the roof was cream fibre glass and there was light inside even with the back doors shut. Obviously it wasn't purpose built. There were no washing facilities and no toilet.

Most sites worldwide have a facility for those needs however and it ran well when Guy had finished with it. The owner was delighted and set off on holiday. Guy went on to mend a huge Removal Lorry next. He was a good engineer and even built gear boxes and engines up. I was full of admiration at his manliness and competence. After Gordon's performance, or lack of it, my head was really turned.

So finally, I decided to leave home when he was abroad doing one of his 'Company' trips. I wasn't brave enough to go when he was there, he would have attacked me. He had already beaten me and thrown me down the stairs when I installed a couple of single beds. I remember landing on the bike stored at the bottom, bits of metal stuck in me, it really hurt. Fortunately I was slim, fit and agile. He could have easily put me into hospital though, I knew that he was only a shade away from doing me real damage soon . . . I had to get away from there.

My colleague Stephanie was a lovely tall Jewish girl, very intelligent and a stunner. She was one of my managers and very capable in everything she did and she volunteered to help me move. She was strong and not easily scared. I didn't want Guy involved, so she and I loaded the van between us. Guy had found a flat that was empty from people he worked for, they had a Rolls Royce and he maintained it. The flat was a council one and they were affluent, so they had decided to buy a house in Bromley. I would continue to pay the rent whilst I looked for somewhere more permanent to rent or the proposed purchase became available. They left behind beautiful Persian carpets and a marvellous chandelier, the very things I loved. My furniture looked wonderful in that flat and I assumed we would have a haven for a while. Things I thought were looking up.

Chapter Twenty Two

I left Gordon frozen dinners in the fridge and half of everything, even a spare vacuum cleaner. I only took what I had been responsible for within the marriage, the things that I had paid for. He couldn't accuse me of anything mean and spiteful. I found out later, that he had put it about that I owed money everywhere, which of course I did not—it was all my earnings that we lived on anyhow. I wasted my kindness on him when I went. I should have taken everything and left debts like he said. I was brought up to have high standards. I would never have considered doing anything wrong. I was just protecting my life and the happiness of my children. Now that he is old, I often wonder if he thinks about the past. I know from relatives that he is rejected by the whole family as he continued to be mean to his daughter. He has even had more affairs; he has never learned. What a truly stupid fellow; if he suffers, I certainly won't be sorry.

Gordon was very churchy, an Altar boy in his youth. He wasn't a good advertisement for religion. Mind you, most of the people that I have ever met who would do as little for you as possible, have purported to be religious. My friend tells me that the Salvation Army helped him in a time of great personal tragedy, he lost a son and it must have been so hard not to lose his mind too. It is nice to be corrected over a thing like this, I personally have had a very unpleasant happening from a member of the 'Sally

Ann.' I guess it isn't the ad more azffairsOrganisation; it is the individual to blame. I was obviously unlucky; I was a child at the time though. I will not recount the instance, it is depressing.

I personally choose to be *'Agnostic'*; therefore, I believe that there is certainly something, the *something* that causes spiritual occurrences. I have had some of these and can't forget them. I do not wish to be told what to believe however, I will make up my own mind and I like 'Humanism', caring for others. Why must people need to be instructed all the time, what is right is obvious and we don't need some droning old cleric in a dress, telling us. I love 'Free Thinkers', I couldn't be a follower, a sheep—if I tried. The planet seems to keep a balance of population with its constant wars, famines and other horrors which keep the numbers down. Humanity always comes up with a solution to vast problems eventually and discoveries get discovered when the time is right, sometimes in two parts of the world at the same time which shows that they were ready to be developed. No one said that humanity is meant to be kind and considerate, wouldn't it be nice if it was. Terrible things happen but life always finds a way. My theories are not comforting to those who want someone to care about them exclusively. It amuses me how people try to buy their way into heaven by leaving fortunes to the church, what a waste—that money could have gone into research to try and curtail cancer and other ghastly diseases. Why don't people try being nicer in their lifetimes instead of trying to make up for it at the end. Life seems to me to consist of 'givers and takers' and there are far too many 'takers' unfortunately.

I have also observed that *most* religions denigrate the female. Recently the *Last Supper*, Leonardo *Da Vinci's* famous fresco, has been the subject of much analysis. Is it a woman next to Jesus on his right? Only a world whose religions hate females so much, could argue about this. Unless the male next to him was wearing womanly garments and bore all the aspects of femininity, *of course it is a woman.* Probably Mary Magdalene his wife. She had been painted out. He had the company of a woman, shock horror. Did you ever hear of anything so ridiculous? The female of the species, which is *50% of it and which also has to produce more of the species,* is considered too disgusting to be featured in the picture. How insulting.

However, I could go on and on about how men denigrate women. Perhaps it is because they fear them. After all, the female out-performs them right at the stage when boys are the most conscious of things and forming their opinions. At the teenage stage, they see the girls doing better at most subjects. They might be the same age, but boys are several years younger where maturity is concerned. True, the males catch up academically later, but the harm is done, even so they are mostly 'little boys' for life.

I know.—Secure men and those brought up to have a good sense of self, will not have any problem with the female sex. I am sure it is all in the upbringing.

Perhaps, all schools should be single sex? The sexes develop at different times. This argument has been raging for years.

I have brought up my boys to be able to do everything in the house. Being 'Hands On' with the children is natural to them. Then again, my daughter services her own car and mends things. 'Role reversal' is quite a useful ability, a partner could die or leave and it helps to be able to cope. It all comes down to education and in many countries they don't educate the female at all. This really enables the males to be Lord of All. Women have no social standing and can't even go out, without a chaperone. They certainly aren't allowed to drive a car. There are many other sad things as well; I can't write them here, it is all too distressing.

This cruelty takes care of the problem very well and in certain countries they ensure that the female can't get sexual gratification either. They cut the sensitive bits off and sew them up. Often the girls die from septicaemia or die in child birth later. Imagine how it would be if men were not allowed to enjoy sex. The poor girls will never experience one of life's fundamental sensations. That 'Joy of living' that feels so good, is *cruelly* denied to them. I don't need to go on about injustice to the female. Some brave souls are trying to do something about it. I wish it could be speeded up, more are suffering every day. Often the old ignorant women think that girls will not get married at all unless mutilated in this way and they wield rusty scissors and razor blades, doing the job themselves. I know for sure, that some British Surgeons used to do operations in this country *secretly* for the wealthy and for all I know, still do. This fact was revealed to me by a member of MI 6. I hope it no longer happens. Remember though, money talks.

Money still seems to rule the conscience. Look at arranged marriages, very young girls have to marry old men who are usually the moneyed ones, because their parents find them useful to bring money into the family through the dowry system—they are business vessels. They pay the families for the daughter's hand, so that they can legitimately come to this country. Spare a thought for these poor girls, who are dragged out of their English schools, having their education stopped and forced to become child brides.

In other countries, girls are used in many sexual ways, by being sold by their parents to pimps or traffickers in the sex trade. There are cases where girls have tried to escape and been murdered by their whole family . . . Mothers, Fathers and Brothers—in *this* country, heaven knows what happens to them in their own. I know that 'Honour killings' are still regularly carried out, money has changed hands for the girl. That is the reality. If she doesn't comply, she is made an example of; it keeps the other girls obedient. It is nothing to do with honour; it's all to do with business and the sale of the girl. Changes seem to be coming about in the U.K. however, thankfully. It is about precious time. After all, it is just fate where one is going to get born, please don't let there be re-incarnation. I might end up somewhere where an opinionated woman and one who doesn't do as she is told, gets punished for it or even killed. Or married off to some old man who smells old—yuk.

Just because women like flowers, fashion, shoes and bags—things that macho men aren't usually fascinated by, doesn't mean that they can't measure up to the occasion when required to do so. From the days of Grace Darling in a rowing boat, helping her father save people in a terrible storm at sea, to the women alongside the soldiers, fighting in trouble spots all over the world in modern times and the heroines in between. Girls are not found wanting.

Chapter Twenty Three

To resume my escape, MY BIGGEST ADVENTURE OF ALL.

Leaving a home after many years is terribly traumatic and needs to be done with the help of a good friend. I had one, Guy . . . he found me and the children, a flat on the eleventh floor of a tower block. I thought it would be fine and we moved the furniture, pets and bikes etc in.

The couple who said that I could have their council flat forgot to mention that they owed lots of rent and that the flat was in the process of being repossessed. I knew there was a little owing. I merrily went down to the Council office pretending to be the owner, with the arrears money and the rent book. I knew that it was illegal, but thought that if I pretended to be her, I could pass a period of time there. The housing officer *knew* that I wasn't the woman in whose name the rent book was. They took the money and then gave me marching orders. I was frightened but they said tough luck, they had workmen coming round to fix the flat up for the next people and we had to get out immediately. I should have known better, I had never lived in a council home, except as a child with our prefab. Mum always paid the rent and I did not know the system. I do not think that it was right that they took the money, maybe they thought that it was from the woman who owed it? I was conned and it was my own fault. It wasn't really a good experience; it was more a 'baptism by fire'. Having to leave that flat was an awful blow, the children were so unhappy—the pets and all our stuff had to go back into storage. Recalling some of my past memories has been pure misery. What I was to discover about my having to wait so long for our home in Nunhead, makes me feel suicidal when I think of it.

In those days it was dangerous to get stuck with tenants . . . they took ages to remove. There was a new rent act that had come out some time earlier, giving all sorts of new rights to the tenant, it worked horribly against me though. There was nothing I could do, I had to go. Knowing what I know now, I should have stayed, they couldn't have thrown a woman and children onto the street—somehow they would have found a place to accommodate us, it might have been dreadful though. Having no phone there, I was worried because I did not know the day that the workmen would come and had they turned up whilst I was taking the children to school, they could have got in and taken all my belongings. Truth was; I wasn't brave enough all on my own, to stay.

I was so pulverised with fright that my ex would find out and get custody of the children. They were an affluent family and there was a sister who would have taken them over joyfully because she couldn't have children herself and was wealthy. She was very fond of them. She told tales and sided with Gordon in every way. She was married, but was having an affair with her husband's workman, Jeff. My husband and his sister had a common bond, they were both adulterers. Before very long, her husband passed away from cancer. He had been a retired policeman in MI 6. They had loads of property and this Jeff maintained it. He was also maintaining her.

I had no idea what was going on and when Jeff tried to lure me into a sexual situation whilst working at our home, I told my sister-in-law what he so licentiously said. You can imagine how that went down. I had no idea that they were lovers, he was ugly and scrawny. She said to me 'You think everyone fancies you'. The damage was done and I knew that old saying, 'revenge is sweet' and she could have had hers with a vengeance.

I was tortured, my mind didn't think logically, it was such a crisis and I couldn't risk him finding out what had happened. Gordon's family kept a solicitor on hand who would have seen that my children went into his and his sisters' care. I could have lost them. Justice was geared towards the male in those days, especially if he had money. I had very little.

I quickly went to the Homeless Families division of the local council. I explained that I was waiting to buy a cottage in Nunhead, but the seller had put it on the market too soon and although it was promised to me, I would have to wait another year before I could take possession.

This particular charming little semi-detached cottage was the place I had to have, according to Guy. It had three garages with electricity and a shed. A greenhouse and a big area of concrete *hard standing* complete with a water tap. There was the hope of Guy running a business at the place and it was perfect.

I expect you wonder how I could to buy a house if I had no serious money. There is a fascinating tale there.

Guy had a mortgage with a well known lender . . . I had no mortgage at all.

Guy and I used to eat lunch in Streatham. It was before I left home and Gordon. The youngsters were at school and I had free time in the day then. We went to a dear little Italian cafe on a corner. A nice girl waited on us, attractive and chatty. We often saw her smiling and talking to a solitary grey haired elderly man in a business suit, in the corner. I asked her if he was someone a bit special. She said that he was the manager of one of the largest Banks in the High Street. They were having a bit of a 'fling'; even though he was actually married . . . I stored the knowledge. No wonder she was so nice all the time. She was happy. At that time as I said, I was still at home with Gordon, I was not.

Guy suggested that he should ask his current mortgage company if they could give him a second one with me, a joint one. When he did, he said they laughed at him. Those were the days when such things were hard to get. If you had one already, you couldn't expect another. He part owned a property already.

Managers had only so many that they were allowed to give out each year, a quota. To have a chance you had to be a saver too. I was not, nor was Guy. We didn't know these facts at the time. So as he had failed at his existing lenders, we strolled along to one of *my* choice and went boldly in. This time, it was me who marched up to the desk and asked for an appointment with the manager. One was duly booked and I was the victim selected to have to go and grovel.

The day came and I dressed in my brown leather mini-skirt and waistcoat, a frilly semi transparent blouse underneath. With long grey suede high heeled boots, I looked pretty nifty. Nothing was actually revealed by my top, but it looked rather sexy. I think that is the secret, don't reveal too much. Wear a look that 'teases.' These days, all is revealed and it leaves nothing to the imagination. At award ceremonies, beautiful women wear dresses that practically, show the lot. The art is to *hint at what lies beneath*. That is what I think, and always will. As I got out of Guy's car, I put my foot down a pothole. My ankle was sprained and my face went white, I felt sick with pain. I felt the ankle filling the boot, it was swelling fast. Guy pushed me forward and said "Go". I staggered out of the vehicle and limped to the mortgage company's door. A young man assisted me to walk up the stairs to the manager's office and I collapsed into a chair. The manager was all sympathy and the ankle was a great ice-breaker. He was a dark curly haired man with 'puppy dog' brown eyes, very good looking and I could tell, knew it. I explained about needing to leave home and why. I also told about my boyfriend who was earning good money and my jewellery selling job. He didn't say no, but asked me if I was a saver. I admitted that I was not but that I could soon become one. He explained the system but didn't refuse me, then and there. He tended to talk looking at my chest, but then most men did. *I used to get asked my bra size a lot in those days*, it is so different now. Equality has stopped the exploitation of women to a certain extent in Britain. Thank heavens. Anyhow, if I could put a sizeable amount into a savings account, he wouldn't turn us down as long as we obeyed the rules and of course he had to meet Guy to look him over. I was rather proud of my performance and informed Guy of my good fortune, who cared about the ankle. He had mixed emotions; he was proud but aware that I could pull off what he couldn't. He swallowed his pride and congratulated me.

Next I tottered across the road to the bank that our waitress told us about. I got another appointment booked, with the manager that I had seen at the cafe. When I attended it, the next morning, he looked at me strangely saying "Haven't I seen you somewhere before?" I simpered and told him about the cafe. I then said, "Eileen sent me along to see you, as I have a bit of a problem." Then I told him about the mortgage offer at the Abbey National and how I had to be a saver. He said he *liquid lunched* sometimes with the manager, at the local pub. They also played golf together. I didn't use his bank alas, but said that if he would lend us five hundred pounds, I would pay the amount straight away to the lender over the road and give him the pass book as security. Eileen would be thrilled at his cooperation, as she was a friend of mine. A bit of a fib, *although she did hold a jewellery party for me once at her place, with her girl friends.* I told him about my life and that I needed to be in a home of my own, where I would be safe.

He was basically kind, although I did rather have him over a barrel. He couldn't afford a scandal. He did not know that I would never tell anyone. Perhaps he too, should have tried being loyal to his wife. So he too said 'Yes' . . . I was saved and took the money over to the mortgage company and paid it in. I was offered a 100% mortgage, such things were available then, imagine. I felt a tad ashamed at all these nefarious actions—but what could a girl do? I had two children to protect, apart from myself. That saying, 'Who dares, wins' . . . it is true, always take a chance and try. Sometimes it works; sometimes not, but at least try. Being an achiever usually takes courage and I had it. Guy must have thought he'd hit pay dirt with me, I was a go-getter.

Chapter Twenty Four

Getting back to my previous story . . . before I told about how I got the mortgage offer.

The Council Homeless Division gave us a room in Pimlico; it was one of their better lettings they said. It was squalid, with the smell of faecal matter outside the window where it had been thrown, and a certainty of bugs in the mattresses. It was run by some Spanish people and it was so filthy that I was afraid to turn the light out at night, in case creepy crawlies attacked us. The next day, Guy drove up to get us, thankfully. We had to find somewhere else and quick.

The children, who saw their father some weekends, had to admit that we had moved from the Tower Block. They said that we were staying at Stephanie's; as I previously mentioned, she was my friend and work colleague. She lived with her sister and husband, quite a distance from Dulwich. Nevertheless, we put toys in the garden and moved them regularly to look as though they had been played with. If he knocked she was to say we were out.

We had the odd bath there as well. She couldn't put us up as she was sharing with family and there wasn't any room. He never knocked however, and didn't seem too anxious to see the children; anyway, I expect he had other interests. When they did see him, he used them to help with his jobs. He was 'smartening' the place up to sell it. After the divorce years later, I got nothing except a shilling a week (which I never received.) appart from a small remuneration for the children, but how much the house was eventually sold for I don't know, it was a huge one in Dulwich though, a very good area. I allowed him to divorce me—even though I could have brought up the cruelty and contested, I didn't bother. I guess I was rather foolish, but I never wanted to see him again. If he is unhappy, he deserves all that life has handed him out as I am told that he is still alive. I doubt that he gets on well with people.

He was messed up completely by a mother who possessed little heart; he was probably not loved as a child. His mother told me that he was an 'accident' in the change of life. *I bet he didn't even know how to love.* She didn't.

He was terrible to the children, there was no taking the kids to nice places or buying treats. They hated going there. I actually found them sitting on pub steps once, with bags of crisps—can you imagine how I felt? I flounced into the pub and told him and his girl, off. He was lucky that I didn't just shove them into my car and drive away. I would probably have been in the wrong if I had done that—I wanted to though. Fury can make one irrational but I never ever left them on pub steps as it is dangerous and appalling.

To continue, we had several disasters and heart breaks getting turned out of various homes. It was like my childhood all over again. The pain of these times is too terrible to put down on paper. Although it would make interesting reading, it is too painful to recall. There was just nowhere for us, the council wasn't interested, we had refused their placing and now we were on our own.

The ex. Bread Van returned from the South of France and some boys had smashed the windscreen. It was too wide to park on the Public Highway. The young fellow, who owned it, offered it to Guy to sell for him. This could be our way out of misery temporarily, Guy recounted our tale of woe and happily he said yes. He didn't want much for it as it needed a windscreen.

We put it at the back of a Freezer store in Penge. It wasn't much of an exulted address, but handy as we had contacts in the area. Out of the garage where a man had let me store my things, came the bunk beds. I had a bit of board across the storage lockers and with a junior mattress on top, it was big enough for me to sleep. We acquired a windscreen and it was all systems GO. We put gas bottles and a camping cooker and fire in and we were snug and considered it our holiday home and a big secret from everyone. We even went down to Cornwall for a fortnight's vacation to amuse the kids and Guy came as well. We made our first stop in Surrey. It was a great laugh and when we eventually arrived in Cornwall, all the people on the campsites where we stayed, gave panicky looks—please do not put it near us. They were in their posh vans and tents and we were a bit of a disaster area in that thing. Guy did redeem himself though. He managed to put out a fire that a woman had in her lovely tent—it could have been very serious had he not been so quick off the mark. We had a great time however, and I made it cute inside. We had proper meals and the children camped outside in a two man tent, as the weather was super. What a holiday it was, it was a chance to be romantic and smooch—a thing I hadn't been able to do for years. The weather was perfect and I sent wonderfully happy cards to mum and my sister from each destination. I couldn't imagine a single cloud on the horizon.

When we drove back to our parking place in Penge, we had the problem of finding somewhere to wash, iron (the kids had school uniforms) and use toilets.

The answer was ingenious, the freezer business had staff and they had a wash room under stairs that led up to flats above the shops. Guy moved the side construction which was flimsy, we slipped through it. The door would still be locked but side entry was easy and inside there was a heater which plugged in, for the hot water and iron. There was a sink of course and a nice loo which locked. It was lovely and clean and seemed for females only. I used to do my ironing on the Sundays—the shop was closed then. I would simply take in the board, unplug the heater and pop my iron on. The sink was also big enough for us to wash our hair. Nobody would have known we didn't have a nice normal home. We were all immaculate with our clothes ironed. The laundrette washed our things. The best thing of all was that the freezer shop had a big extractor fan which blew out warm air and when I stood on the van's steps, I could dry my long hair in the warm current of air blowing out. It was a hot summer that year but could get chilly at night in the van, as it was metal. When the night came, I transferred the gas hose onto the heater and warmed the place up before we went to bed. We ate a lot in the cafe across the road, inexpensive Italian food which saved cooking and prevented the frequent replacement of bottled gas, which I found irksome. The fitting of them was quite a tricky operation, but I managed.

One funny but potentially worrying occurrence happened. I was in the loo minding my own business, when I heard a key in the lock. A girl came in to use the facilities, she had stayed late for some reason. I had to shout "Won't be a minute" and when I emerged through the door her face was a study. I explained everything, I had too. She looked sympathetic and I begged her not to tell her boss. She was as good as her word, I heard nothing from anyone but for a day or two, my nerves were shocking.

After that happened, I felt a bit vulnerable. I wasn't as safe as I thought. Shortly after that, I was to nearly burn us down.

Chapter Twenty Five

It was a weekday morning. The children were at school and I was alone. The weather was glorious and I had made friends with the local ginger Tom. He was visiting for a cuddle and possible titbit or two. I decided to cook some food for lunch and disconnected the pipe from the heater bottle to fix it onto the bottle that I used for the cooker. The lighted match was ready in my hand. *I forgot to switch off the first bottle*. There was instant ignition. A jet of flame shot out singeing my eyebrows and cooking the end of the wooden bunk beds. The cat tried to climb the metal walls and I tried to pull across the sliding door partition and get into the cab and safety. I thought any minute the whole bottle would explode, and in fact, it could have. I was in terror and screaming. The door wouldn't slide across letting me out, it was stiff at the best of times and I was weak with panic. Guy, who was working on his friend's lorry at the other end of the alley, heard my screams and when he looked he could see the flames reflecting through the fibreglass roof. He ran towards the van giving a good impression of the four minute mile. He reached in through the back door; put his hand under the flame and simply turned off the bottle. He said that it wouldn't have exploded, but at the time—I couldn't be sure. It had charred the bed ends and the side of my hair. When he took me into his arms, I was a shaking wreck. After a cup of tea and a bit of comfort, I recovered, it shook me though. Suddenly I was aware that there was real danger in that situation. Luckily it all ended okay, but soon there was to be a much more frightening experience for me to endure . . .

Summer had progressed and it was early autumn. We were still camping in our makeshift home. It was a weekend again and I was alone. Further down the alley was the back of a kebab shop, the boys used to leer at me sometimes and I hoped that they didn't know that I was living that way and near to them. One night, late, I decided to go early to bed and read. Firstly I would go into my dark little cloakroom and clean my teeth etc. I was in my nightdress and dressing gown.

When I emerged from the van I thought I saw a shape in the dark further along the alley; it was pitch black there. I hoped it was my imagination. Needing to go in quickly and get ready for the night, I carried out my little routine. When I emerged to go into the van and shut the door, I was sure that there was someone inside. Frightened, I didn't dare look—there was no light on and I felt terribly threatened. For a moment I stood rigid. Then I had a brainwave, I could get into the garden of Steve, the Fireman—it lay alongside the alley. He did shift work I knew because I used to notice lights go out and his car drive off. His garden had a gate that I could slip through and I was hoping that he was there. I did not have my handbag or any torch with me and mobile phones were not in general use. I had spoken to Steve only once when Guy fixed his car. I crept up to his back door and knocked, but he was out.

What should I do? There was nothing that I could do really, so I found a bench seat on his lawn and settled down. Hours later and shivering, after several cats and a fox had inspected me, covered with dew and desperate for a cup of something hot to ease my stiff and aching joints (how do Tramps sleep in parks?) I saw a light in his kitchen and went and knocked again. He was so surprised. It wasn't what you expect in the small hours from your garden. He recognised me and I told him the story, he took me into the warm kitchen and made me a cup of tea. He was kind and didn't chuck me out. It was a bit unconventional having a strange girl for a guest at that hour, all damp from the dew and scared to death. He picked up his fireman's axe and went to look around the van. He didn't find anything, no sign of an intruder— do you think I suffered all that for nothing? In a way I hoped so, I did not want to think that those boys knew I was there. He got my handbag, closed the door to make the van safe and tucked me up on his sofa. The next day, Guy turned up and wondered where I was, so early in the morning. When I appeared, we shared the tale. I didn't want to go back into the van another night, it was too unnerving even though the children would be back. We went over to the cottage that we were hoping to buy at Nunhead and begged the Vendor to hurry and told her how the children and I were forced to live. She told us a terrible story.

She and her old Gentleman friend, who mended watches, owned a Victorian house in Wandsworth Road. It was a main road in South London. They filled it with Vagrants and the Council paid the rent. One old guy got drunk and there was a fire, several were killed. Despite nobody caring for these old folk, suddenly there was the chance of compensation. From out of nowhere, relatives arrived to sue. My old lady who had housed them didn't have the right kind of insurance and she became the subject of a huge court case. I don't know what the outcome was, but I think that she ended up severely penalised.

She asked me to take her beloved cat Corky. When I said I would of course, she bought me a case of tinned cat food as a thank you. I loved cats and was genuinely pleased to. It broke my heart when he reached his little paws up to the window at the side of her car when she was going to drive away; he knew that he wouldn't see her again. He had many happy years with me though and eventually Mother. She adored him. What is better than a companion to greet you when you are living alone, it makes the house nice to come back to after you've been out. He looked a bit rough when I took him on, the Vendor smoked cigars and he had a juicy chest. He became much better in a non smoking household however. His fur became smooth and silky in clean air and brushing it, made him into a little Prince.

Anyhow, before we finally moved to the cottage, after a short period with the van in another location, the kids and I spent some time living in a house with a newly single Scotsman. He was waiting for his divorce. I had to do the cooking and housework but it was a fraught place because his estranged wife hated me and the kids and kept calling at strange hours, to see if there was something going on. I expect that as she had fancied him once, she thought that he was going to be fancied by another woman and she was protecting her child allowance. She could not have been more wrong, he was revolting and she was worse. I couldn't wait to get away from there—the hygiene was shocking in the house, unhappy marriages never make for interested housewives. I tried hard to make inroads on the squalor. The toilets were nastier than public ones. The kitchen was a health hazard. We survived but only just.

Then my Conveyancing solicitor gave me the good news, the vendor was ready to complete on the cottage. I wept for joy.

What Guy finally did with the van I didn't ask, I was too grateful to see the back of it. It had served a purpose. It made me realise that those who live in their cars, need all the help they can get. I knew a girl who parked on an allotment. She had parents who had washed their hands of her, what her nights had been like I shudder to think. She had strayed a bit in her teenage years and got pregnant. Her parents looked after her little boy, because she was taking something, I don't know what.

Chapter Twenty Six

These things were not the best, but the alcohol consumption of the parents, made things a million times worse. To endure teenagers without going mad, you don't need to be a drunk. It sure makes things a thousand times worse. I knew them all, they kept one of the local shops. They were what one would call 'Beautiful People'. The girl looked divine, a real beauty. Her brother, played rugby and was handsome. The parents, wealthy and secure with their business, were also good looking people. I always envied them, as then, I was loveless and unhappy with Gordon. Of course, I didn't know the half of what was really going on in that house.

Few teenagers seem to get through puberty without making their Mum and Dad crazy. Don't turn to alcohol as that girl's mother did, it definitely makes a bad situation worse. I do not know what happened to her, it all went 'pear shaped' at the same time, that I left Gordon and the area. All I know is that the much preferred brother, committed suicide. Something had taken away his need to live. That was the shocking thing that happened just before I left. After that, maybe they tried to save their poor daughter? If you drink heavily as a parent, it de-stabilises everyone around you.

Yes, my van was a purpose adapted one, but I know for a fact, that many poor souls haven't an adequate spot to pass the night and keep their things in. I wish people were kinder and thought of others more.

After leaving my first married home, when the flat we found didn't work out, many people I knew, who knew quite well at the time that we were in a pickle, failed to offer a room to me and the children. We would have paid them and been so grateful and would never have forgotten it to our dying day. When people are so comfy, they often forget others who are less fortunate—often through no fault of their own. It wasn't as though they would have been stuck with us, we were buying a house and they knew it.

Later in my life, I was able to help in a very positive manner, *two unfortunate folk* who would probably have died otherwise. I shall speak of that later.

After the children and I moved to our little cottage, we thought life in our new home was fantastic. We had to scrape a bit to make ends meet and pay the mortgage, but I was able to start selling again having found a *wholesale warehouse* that sold clothes, in the Old Kent Road.

The young owner, Bobby was related to a firm of retail giants. He was a very nice family man. He heard my story and as I had been a manager selling jewellery in the past, he allowed me some credit and I was off.

Bobby had such lovely things; some were samples and not all of them clothes. There were trainers and many other assorted goods. It was like an 'Aladdin's cave.' I walked around choosing items to sell, totally thrilled. I did a roaring trade in jeans, silk shirts, trainers and even Burglar Alarms. I wasn't greedy and trade was fast and furious. The Croydon police bought a lot, especially the plain clothes detectives who had to sprint fast. I loved going there and I made good friends.

Everything I sold was reasonably priced. Why do people put such 'mark-ups' on things? I realise they have overheads, but the prices could be more reasonable and then we could buy more and they would still make huge profits. It reminds me of the biblical saying, about *a rich man having trouble getting into heaven, it being easier for a camel to pass through the eye of a needle.* Having met several rich men, I can well believe that. I am not religious but it makes sense, greed is a sin. The 'mark-ups' on beds and most consumer items is shocking. Folk fell over themselves to buy my stock. I will never forget the face of a young man who purchased his first smart suit to do his job interviews in, from me at Herne Hill. He had discovered my stall in a side road and he couldn't believe his luck as it was a stylish *sample* and just his chest and waist size. I hope it worked for him. I even put a little stall outside my local shops. The Police came and moved me on—one of the shops rang the police and reported me. I may have sold something that they sold. I noticed that one of the shops carried a bit of everything in it and even did burials as well. I had a mortgage and three children by then. That seemed to cut no ice in business, there is little heart where profit is concerned. I didn't know about trader's licenses . . . was my face red. I decided to go all out. I had proved that I could sell the stuff, why not be legal, so I got a licence. Soon Bobby was upping my credit because I was doing so well. I even got a couple of my previous jewellery selling girls to help also.

They supplied the nurses in the hospitals, as they were nurses themselves. I made enough to buy lots of lines to stock my stall, also cushions and pretty things. I went to a couple of commons, Peckham Rye and Wandsworth Common. They were having 'Fun' days and people put their stalls out—including me. Sun shone and I enjoyed myself, as well as that, I made quite a bit of money because there were so many people there. I also had a stall in Penge market for a while; it was odd being back there. It was the area I had lived in, when I had the bread van.

After Guy came to live with us, I would spend a long hard day working in Penge market on the stall. Guy would come and help me take it down and put it in the vehicle he was driving. He was often late. I assumed he was working hard. We didn't seem to be making much with the car business. I wondered why trade was so poor; he was after all, a very skilled mechanic. I found him several customers who bought his cars, where was the money going? Guy mended vehicles on the area of concrete at the back of the cottage. We had running water out there and plenty of room.

He had previously, before I was with him, rented a petrol station with a partner in Kent, but the relationship ended. He left it, with just his tools—no money. Eventually I discovered why. He was sleeping with the partner's wife and stealing petrol from the business. Ignorance is bliss they say. I did not know what had been happening in the past and what was going on then.

I was so in love and so thrilled to own my first home and to have a burgeoning business. Disillusionment came later, much later.

Chapter Twenty Seven

My belongings had weathered the moves and storage in various garages etc. quite well. There had been some rats gnawing on the feet of my antique dining chairs, but nothing that couldn't be restored. The books were not damp and my lovely furniture, mostly antiques, looked charming mixed with the new acquisitions. The long oak bookcase fitted against the longest wall and added class to the whole look. We didn't have a television, I had left Gordon ours, but Guy bought us one for the first Christmas—it was second-hand, and we loved it. Deprived of television for such a long time, it was thrilling.

I wouldn't have called the Lord Mayor my Uncle . . . I was so proud of our little cottage. We had to get rid of the old green felt fitted carpeting; it was smelly, the previous occupier smoked cigars. We put silver-grey carpeting down, inexpensive stuff meant for a bedroom but with underlay and with the red Bukhara Persian rug that I owned already, it all looked very elegant. The dining end had a 'chunky' pine dining table which I had found being sold, whilst on my travels. It was thick and gorgeous and with my rather super dining chairs in matching pine; I was a Queen in her castle. I had two receptions and a galley kitchen. I didn't mind the lack of kitchen space a bit, I put in a small folding table and a couple of stools for the children, there was a luxurious amount of room after a bread van. My Mother came for Christmas and gave it the thumbs up.

Eventually Guy and I lived together, he came to us and we were thrilled. Our family really felt complete and we decided to have a baby. I was thirty six and delighted to be pregnant. I drove a sports car by then and was working hard. Sadly I miscarried at five months and had to put a hold on activities at the warehouse. I didn't let myself go into a decline over the baby.

I did have a nasty time in hospital though, when a junior Medical student (*it was a teaching hospital*) was practising and accidently perforated my womb. No one would tell me anything, I awoke to find myself on a drip, unable to have anything but ice on my lips. I thought they had found cancer. The young man came and told me the truth, he was so sorry. I must have bled badly because there was blood under my toe nails, I bet chaos reigned. The young man was Chinese. He said that as he was doing it, the instrument 'just seemed to be drawn in'. Anyway, I didn't sue them. He and the hospital would almost certainly have lost any action. That would have resulted in his being kicked out. The "Takeaway" would have been his future and I couldn't condemn him to that.

I recovered slowly but was told that we could try for a baby again, after a year had passed. The worst part was that when I sneezed, a terrible pain would shoot in my side, I think that something had become adhered there somehow. After a long time, it seemed to ease and I felt normal. All my life though, I have had that spot in my tummy as a weak spot. For years, if I was unwell, I always got a sore ache there.

Soon I was well enough, so I became pregnant again. I rested more this time and all went well. I had to have a Caesarean Section as the baby was a whopper. My feet are very small and I was told that they are in relation to the size of the area the baby will pass through, in the process of being born. Thank heavens I was in hospital.

My first two babies were born at home . . . in those days, home births were the thing and fortunately they were both small babies. Giving birth to my first son though, took three days. When he at last was born, he looked terribly poorly and shocked. Foolishly I was determined to have him at home. However, this time I was thirty eight, I was safe in East Dulwich hospital.

A petite woman in jeans with an American accent, who was the surgeon, rushed me down to theatre. Low and behold, there he was. A beautiful, smooth, unwrinkled baby boy, without a hair on his head, *much like he is now at thirty odd.* He really was the talk of the hospital and all sorts of people came to see him. I guess that at my advanced age—I was positively geriatric according to the doctor, and his looking so mature and bonny—it *was* a bit of a sensation. Of course, he is completely fashionable now; men shave off all their hair at the first sign of receding hairlines. The 'slap head' style as I call it is everywhere. The baby was handsome though, as was his father and we were proud. He looked weeks older when he was born and turned out later, to have an exceptional IQ. He could read and write at four, he was very easy to bring up. His daddy seemed to adore him too, as a baby. How sad it was, that women and sex became more important to him than the love of his child.

He was very helpful as a child when things changed dramatically in our lives. He gave great joy to my mother amongst other things, when times were tough for her with her cancer. She helped him to have an interest in classical music and encouraged the piano. He was also first violin in the school orchestra as well as piano soloist. Annoyingly though, he became crazy about computers and gave up music to study them, becoming very talented in that direction. He has currently made them his life's work and works abroad. Our kids usually do what *they* want and not what the doting parents expect. After all, it is true, that being happy is the most important thing.

I must tell you about the fortune teller. I didn't believe in such things. I do now.

When Mother discovered that she had cancer, I decided to go see an old lady in Camberwell. My girl friend said she and her actress friends used to visit for a reading. This old lady lived in a council flat with a little old boyfriend of advanced years. She was so sweet and not a bit scary.

I took Mother and my daughter along, as I knew that she would never say anything tactless regarding her health, even if she saw something. She might well say something nice, to cheer her up. Mum went in first. We had to give her something personal to hold and then she lay cards down with great speed. They were ordinary cards, not Tarot. Firstly, she staggered my Mum by saying that she could see that there was something wrong with her stomach. She said that she would recover and have lots of years of life left. She also said that she saw Mum in a long black skirt and white blouse, playing the piano in front of a lot of people in a big place.

Mother, who was shy and anti-social in her later years, would never play to large numbers. She didn't have the chance anyway.

The lady also said that there was a boy who meant an awful lot to her and was very close. She wondered if it was a grandson or nephew. At that time, Mum only had two grandsons, one was my sister's young teenager in Canada and the other was my teenager. Neither fitted the description she provided us with.

We scratched our heads trying to work that one out. *Would you believe it . . .* I eventually had the son who lived in the same house as her, he became incredibly close and she adored him.

At that time, I was still living with my husband and we were in separate rooms, let alone separate beds. It could only have been a Virgin Birth, if I was the provider of the '*boy to be.*' Also I met an old Chap when selling my jewellery, who used to be a show business 'dresser.' He was putting on a pantomime and needed a pianist. He talked me in to recruiting Mum to help him. They re-arranged sheet music and after rehearsals, lo and behold—when all was ready, Mother played to three hundred people in a big hall. She wore a long black skirt and a white blouse. Everything this fortune teller told Mum was to take place. The timing was a bit wrong that was all. Mum even got over her mastectomy and lived for a further ten years, when in those days, five was considered a cure. She was a founder member to be given Tamoxifen, a wonder drug then which removes the body of oestrogen which of course assists cancer. The cancer eventually graduated (via the lymph nodes) to the liver, so the stomach was eventually involved, but she had a good life in the bosom of the family and passed away at home in her sleep, with her daughter and granddaughter at her side.

I was told that I would be having another son. 'Rubbish' said I—however, years later, I jolly well did . . . SPOOKY.

One other curious event in the same *genre* happened to me later and in a very different phase of my life. I must recount it now . . .

Chapter Twenty Eight

I was in my forties. My last child was quite young. Mum and I, were visiting a family friend and her little daughter in Malvern. She was the final person to have Shandy. I took mum for a country break; it was very beautiful by the river Severn. My male partner, who I had known for quite a long time, drove down for the weekend as well.

I was walking with my Mother, my friend and my little son, along a tow path at the side of the river Severn. I wore a dress ring on my left ring finger. My friend, who had become rather moody and strange recently, was also along for the walk, as I said, he was there visiting just for a couple of days. At that time, he seemed a bit distant, but not at the 'goodbye' stage. I hadn't realised how untrustworthy he was with other women and I was still fond of him.

My child had run along almost out of sight and it was obviously dangerous because we were by water. My pal ran ahead to catch him up. Along the path in the other direction came two ladies. As they came up to Mum and me, they stopped to talk. The one enquired whether that was my fiancé ahead, obviously seeing my ring . . . I said laughing 'No, this is just a dress ring'. She astonished me by remarking that she was thankful, because he had got a dreadful Aura. I was shocked—firstly, what a thing to say, I could have loved him like mad. I didn't as it happened.

Secondly, how could this *Aura* thing be true? I had heard talk of *Aura's* but usually from people *away with the fairies*. I said 'Is mine alright?' She said that it was fine but most definitely, **his** was not. *Do you know, he was to end up committing heinous and criminal acts. He went to jail for a long time.*

We had long since split up fortunately. After all the kindness that he had showed to my family and me in the past, he dumped me for another woman with four boys. He made their lives very dreadful eventually, after they married and had another child.

Isn't it strange how that woman saw what I couldn't, she had the gift—I did not. I will never think that there is NOTHING ever again. What with people seeing in to the future, ghosts and near death experiences. It is just too convenient to dismiss all things spiritual, as nothing.

Many years ago, when I was just a girl, I had heard a tale concerning my Aunty Barbara, my Mum's sister. I dismissed it at the time, as a myth created by Grandma. She loved to put the 'spooks' up us all. Apparently when she was first married, they rented an old house in London. Aunty was a small child. Grandma sent her little daughter into the front room to fetch her sewing basket. Aunty returned without it, crying noisily. Upon enquiring, Grandma discovered that her child had entered a room quite different and all grey and misty. There on the floor was a woman kneeling—in old fashioned dress. A man (presumably her husband) stood behind her, strangling her. It was a terrifying sight and so convinced was Grandma; that she had the place checked out. Only to find, that YES, there *had* been a murder there once, some years previously. A husband *had* despatched his poor wife and in that very room.

What can be said about this? Maybe Grandma and her first daughter both had the second sight. I am glad that I have not. Seeing ghosts would scare me silly, I am not brave. I should make sure that I lived the perfect life though, if I did. My Grandmother didn't live a good life, maybe there is some sort of retribution after the grave? It puts me in a quandary, I want her punished—yet she is my Grandmother, I also want her forgiven and shown what she did that was wrong, what is the point of punishment, if one doesn't realise what it is for.

Life with Guy, in our cottage was varied and interesting. I got on with the lady next door, she was odd but nice. She lived alone and was very dirty. I later found out that she had no water. She had been turned off, for owing the authorities money. They have ceased that practise now thankfully; she was unable to control her life. She suffered from a mental illness and had bad leg ulcers which smelled awful. She lived alone, just with hoards of dogs and cats. She chain smoked so probably didn't realise how bad the smell was.

In warm weather, large blow flies would emerge from her back door and fly into my kitchen. I sprayed them with insecticide . . . bad for all of us, but I didn't realise just how bad in those times.

She was taken by the police who arrested her, when I was out one day. They took her to Holloway Prison. The dogs went to Battersea Dogs home. I realised that they would treat her legs and clean her up. I decided to phone the prison and asked them to tell her that I would feed the cats every day, whilst she was gone. It also gave us a chance to look through the lace curtain into her front room. There on the floor was a decaying dog. No wonder there were large blow flies.

I realised that as she had filled each room with squalor, she moved into the next. She used the empty dog food cans as receptacles to hold urine and stacked them up on top of each other. They were floor to ceiling. As you can imagine, the ones at the bottom of the pile, were rusting and gave way as they were taken from the pile for pouring into the plastic dustbin (which served as a holding tank) prior to disposal. All other waste she had dug into the back garden and hidden in drawers wrapped in old newspaper. The house was rank. No wonder there was a lack of the scent of flowers coming from her garden.

She had been given a written warning to clean it as it was a health hazard, she couldn't handle the situation as she was not well in the head. We had a baby in our house and I was worried. Before she was taken to Holloway, I had no idea how bad it was. She couldn't touch anything dead. There were several dead birds in a cage under a pile of mess. When the animals got sick, she just left them. She was tragic and her husband died from a perforated ulcer, maybe the poor man could have been saved. She probably didn't want anyone to see into her filthy house. He wasn't old, if only she had called the hospital sooner maybe. I did not know everything, as it was long before my time, but I can guess. These people should not be left alone to try and survive, they are tragic cases and it is not the dark ages.

Before we discovered all these dreadful facts about her, Christmas was coming and I felt concern for this lonely lady. She wasn't old but she was abandoned. I decided to invite her for a Christmas dinner. I asked the children and Guy, they grudgingly said yes. She was overjoyed and cleaned herself up to an extent. Her hair was tidied and she had clean dressings on her legs. I promised the family that I would clean the leather sofa and armchair thoroughly and spray it with bug killer. She enjoyed a drink or two and we gave her presents from the tree. She had a lovely day being made a fuss of. It was to stand me in good stead later.

I still did my jewellery job, but along with my clothes selling. I had several girls working for me. They had cases of sample jewellery. When they weren't selling enough or were losing interest, I had to fire them. I had to drive to their houses and get their samples back.

One afternoon I was driving past Battersea Park, having collected a girl's samples from her, in the Battersea area. As I passed one of the entrances, who did I see but this neighbour with all her dogs, emerging from the gateway. She had picked them up from the dog's home, having been released from jail. She had taken them to the park for a call of nature. I screeched to a halt, I was driving a van that day and said 'Can I give you a lift?' She looked delighted and I loaded all the dogs in the back and her in the front.

How strange was that? I never drove over that way usually and rarely took the old van. As we drove along, I asked her if all her debts were now eradicated. She said that she still had to pay. I couldn't believe it; she had done time and yet still owed money. As we continued, I told her about my Mother's mobile home. I told her how lovely the site was and how the dogs would love wandering in the nearby woods if they were there. I told about the site facilities, the bath block and the club house.

I needed my Mum to be on hand because of her hospital appointments, it was a long drive to fetch her for Kings College hospital. I said that we could turn the two semi detached houses into one. There would be room for my two sons and my daughter. My Mother could stay as long as she needed, it would be wonderful. There would be much less work and driving for me.

I suggested that if I paid off all her debts and moved her to the van, looking after her bills and keeping an eye on her, would she consider selling us the house cheap? She said that she would give the idea serious consideration.

She later told me that she was about to desert the house and take to the road with her dogs, becoming a travelling lady. How long could she have lasted like that? I guess that I was a last ditch alternative for her, I just did not realise it at that time.

I decided to take her down to see the van and site the following Sunday. Mum said that she would make sandwiches and tea in the garden, as we were having lovely weather. She didn't want too much of her smell, which was back by then, in the house.

She so loved the van and the marina. She said it would be ideal for them. Mother, although very reticent, could see the sense of being somewhere more substantial and closer still to me. I realised that the giving up of the van that she had made so beautiful would be a wrench, she had been burgled though and living alone without the protection of dogs, was a bit scary when one was elderly. So my neighbour, Mum and I agreed a small price and threw in the van and all the other benefits as part of the deal.

We had a job getting her to actually make the move; she didn't want us to see the state of the house. She didn't know that we had looked. Eventually she was persuaded by me that we would tell no one, whatever we found.

We had a large quote from the council to send in the cleaning department. It was huge. It turned out that we had to do it ourselves anyway; the bin men and cleaning section went on strike. We had no choice, so the kids, Guy and I, dressed in boiler suits and with surgical masks on, set to.

It was a horrid job and took days. I will not go into detail except to say that when my daughter with a scarf over her mouth, was on a step ladder, knocking through the upstairs ceiling, prior to it being re-plastered, a great profusion of maggots fell down all over her. It was fortunate they missed going into her open mouth, as she was talking. This was 'Celebrity Get Me out of Here.' in real terms, many years before it was thought of . . . *a pigeon had perished up there.* We had to laugh. You could hear her screams up the road.

We had to spend a lot of money making it habitable. We even had to get a staircase made. The roof was in good order though and most of the windows were whole. Local kids had smashed a couple of them at the back and of course there was no bathroom.

When it was nearly finished, we had run out of money. I suggested that we temporarily let it to a couple of students. A gay girl we knew, suggested a gay couple, as they would take good care of it. She advised me to ring 'Gay Switchboard.' They were always looking for good places to let.

I duly phoned them. The phone call caused great mirth. The person on the other end couldn't speak for laughing when I said that I had a nice cottage for rent with two bedrooms. I was puzzled, what had I said? When he stopped laughing, he told me that *'Cottaging'* was a practice often carried out by certain gay people. It was when they *visited public toilets for procuring partners.* He didn't explain quite so modestly . . . CRIPES. Enough said on that subject.

Chapter Twenty Nine

We found two nice young men who, I am sure didn't have weird lifestyles. They just loved each other and any love is good love, by my thinking. I am not here to moralise and it would be cruel to deny people who are born gay, a life without sex.

They cannot be cured and usually wouldn't want to be. I think that the *style* of lovemaking upsets heterosexual folk very often. The practise of love making 'The French way,' which was what it used to be called in this country. Probably the *'English Way'* in France. This style has been practised by most people since time began, to avoid pregnancy. Why is there such hypocrisy? What you get up to in bed, as long as it doesn't frighten the horses as they say, is fine. Just do not involve children or animals. That is a sin by anyone's reckoning. Also, consider the danger of wrecking muscle tone which will cause problems in old age. By and large though, the fabulous exercise that *bonking* gives, loses tons of fat and is the best diet I know.

Visiting my ex-neighbour in Hoo was always a joy. Guy refused to come with me. He was never nice to her. He just didn't have common decency or a heart. He was quite shocking, as I was to find out soon.

One day when I went through to the garages to take him a mug of tea, I noticed that the rear side window of his car was messy. As though a big dog had hung his head out of the window, in the way that big dogs do and slobbered a bit. I didn't remark about it, I was so secure in our love and we had our son by then. He used to go and help daddy work and lose all the spanners. I loved my life, it was busy but we were making ends meet.

I had the responsibility of the ex. neighbour in Mother's old mobile home and my promise to her, which I was carrying out.

I also kept rabbits for my daughter, she adored them. I had a house bunny called Snuffles, she loved Bacardi and Coke. Her mother rabbit had put her outside the nest, she was ill with breathing problems but I didn't realise at the time. She was a sweet rabbit, but she didn't survive long. We were rather overrun with rabbits, my little girl used to show the two best. They were Black Alaska's and they won Trophies for her. She also used to subscribe to the 'Fur and Feather' magazine. She was very serious about her hobby. Her letters to the magazine were hilarious and cute. She was crazy about animals like me.

One day Guy told me that he had bunged up a hole in a wall, in which a bumble bee had crawled. I was mortified, why did you do that? He laughed, 'It's only a Bee' he said. I wept at the senseless cruelty of it. How could a person do such a thing? He was to do much more.

He was re-pointing the chimney with a builder friend when our cat climbed up the ladder rungs and joined them on the roof. Guy was seen by my older son to pick the cat up and throw him to the ground. He survived the fall; it must have shaken him though. My son being afraid of what telling me would cause to happen, kept quiet about this. Consequently, I had no idea that he had turned against our animals. First it was to be them and then next the two older children. Next was to be me.

I was in complete ignorance that he was having sex with a woman, who lived in the road parallel to ours. She had a dog and two children. He was taking them out for country trips and no doubt, lunches.

The next strange happening was that this woman's teenage daughter was mugged at the bus stop. She had her bracelet taken by some black girl. There were many bad happenings in the borough of Peckham. She arrived in tears at our garage, where Guy was working. Why did she know to come crying to him I thought? Her mother was at work, so I took her into my kitchen and comforted her. I gave her some of the sample jewellery that I sold, to replace that which had been stolen. One of the items, a necklace was called 'Gift of Love.' Ironic really, she was old enough to know that I was Guy's other half and we had a small child. I had given her a necklace and a matching bracelet. She took them. I taught my children to have a moral conscience from a young age, this child was about thirteen or fourteen, she should have known better than to accept my kindness when she knew what her mother and Guy were up to. No doubt she would have grown up to behave in the same disgusting manner as her mother and for all I know she has wrecked relationships without a second thought as well. She couldn't help what her mother did, but she didn't have to take my jewellery and come crying at our garage as though Guy was single and connected to her family.

One Sunday, we took the little one to a local artificial lake, and who was there but this woman Jane, her child and dog. I had never known that the lake was even there, in the Camberwell area. It must have all been arranged by Jane and Guy. Jane wore a new pretty dress which she told me her boyfriend had bought for her, she was flaunting it and so proud. I had no idea that it was my man. He was the boyfriend. They had been having an affair for ages. I remembered then seeing her at the garage a couple of times. I had assumed he was fixing her motor. The penny just hadn't dropped properly. Even now, there is pain when I recount these happenings, I was so happy and unsuspecting, what shockers they were.

Winter came and the snow fell. Guy, the kids and I, made a large snowman on the pavement out at the front. It was a through road, but very little used. It was rare that any one walked in front of our house, apart from meter readers and the postman. I assumed that the snowman was for our three children and we dressed it up. I expect 'Guy's other family' came around to see it, when the children and I were out shopping. There were masses of footprints, they weren't all ours.

I owned a lovely sleigh and he pulled me and our young child, through the old unused cemetery around the corner. The trees looked wonderful and it was like fairy land. I felt such happiness, little knowing that later, that place would have a special horrific meaning to me.

Spring arrived and Mother's appointments kept me busy. She was under Kings College hospital.

Directly across the road from Kings, was the Maudsley Psychiatric hospital. It used its car park to hold car Boot Sales. I regularly put a stall out with old toys, books and musical instruments that the kids had outgrown etc.

One Sunday, I saw an obvious mental patient who was wandering round the sale looking at the stalls. He was a large black man with a strange blond wig on and what looked like flour all over his face. He was a strange sight and my daughter and I had a discreet smile together.

Annie Scott

The following Sunday I felt tired and decided not to get up at the early hour, to put my little table out. It was lucky for me. This same patient bought a knife off one stall and cut the throat of a girl at another. They saved her thankfully, Kings College hospital being over the road, a transfusion 'saved the day.' What a terrible happening, it could have been me. Only I was so unlucky, I would have died. I gave up Boot Sales.

Whilst we were living in Nunhead, Guy came enthusiastically in one day telling me that I had to go to see a house, that was cheap and on the market. He had insider knowledge and told me that there was one old lady living on the middle floor. She was about to leave to live with her sister, who had already gone. I did not ask him how he knew all about this, I assumed that he was just mooching around the estate agents locally and looking at properties.

We went to see it and the old lady confirmed that she was only temporary. It was a nice large Victorian house on three floors, but in a less than fashionable area. Nevertheless, I could envisage tenants in the rooms and space for my growing children one day.

We still hadn't knocked the wall through into next door, combining the two cottages into one. It was proving to be a bit of a squeeze.

The situation of this big house was right by the South Circular road at Tulse Hill. The back of the garden looked across a pub car park, to the South Circular. It doesn't sound all that nice a location, but it was. It was spacious.

It had a surprisingly big garden, with trees. I had to admit that the house was spectacular.

It was arranged into three sections, the top and bottom being empty. It wouldn't normally have been

150

possible to obtain a mortgage for this house under normal circumstances. However, I had a friend, the Manager of the Abbey building society. He was approachable, as Guy had recently sold him an inexpensive little car for his daughter. He seemed very pleased with it.

I went to see him and he sanctioned the mortgage, but only if it was in my sole name. I worried about what Guy would say, but he was surprisingly tolerant. I think he knew that it had to be that way, or not at all.

Yes, with a minimal deposit, we could pay for it out of the rents obtained from the tenants. We were in the right place at the right time. We were also lucky, that he liked us both.

Thank goodness things have changed now; managers had so much power then. In fairness, I expect that I said that our house was too small and we had Mum and the growing children to accommodate and that of course, was true. I doubt if we mentioned the tenants that we were going to obtain, we couldn't have managed the mortgage without them.

After we bought it, Guy filled it with nurses from Kings. I helped them with their pre-exam swotting and in the main they were nice girls. They, being young had never lived away from home before. I felt quite proud pretending to be an examiner and firing off questions.

Only one of the mothers came and looked us and the house over. Had it been me, I should have wanted to know how my girl was going to be living. Funnily enough, her daughter was the one whose toe nails rattled all the way up the Hoover's metal pipe, when I cleaned under her bed after she had left, to take up her first nursing post. These girls were provided with a bus for holidaying in by Guy, painted with rude slogans on the side. I did not know any of this until later. I was shocked at the lifestyle of the girls. I suppose, work hard . . . play hard.

One of the senior girls, she became a Staff Nurse, was becoming very friendly to me. She had a nice older brother called Mike, who also became friendly with my son. The lads would do gardening and fencing together for pocket money, whilst my son finished his sixth form.

Unbeknown to me, this lovely girl was having an affair with Guy.

He seemed to have so many females on the go at once. I found women usually rather *catty* to me, no surprise there then. He was probably bedding them. Although the Staff Nurse was nothing but funny and sweet—I should have like to have had her friendship for life. She went off to Australia and it wasn't until then, that I found out about them. I eventually also found out about FOUR girls. He was having sex with them all. No wonder he kept me busy cooking for him, he needed the calories . . .

He had a shocking track record, but I didn't know such 'sex addicts' existed then. He told me in the past, when he was after me, about the partner's wife. That he had accumulated nothing with his stupid behaviour. He had learned his lesson. He wanted me and my children and a regular decent life.

I forgave the past and foolishly thought we could have just that. Leopards cannot change their spots however, he made no changes. *He was a big liar.* He used me as a respectable procurer of property, tenants, and all the nice things we had. He just slept with most of the females we knew.

It was a miracle I did not get something nasty, there was Aids and other horrors then, as indeed there still are. He didn't use a condom with me, how could he? It would have been a dead giveaway. I was very lucky not to get a terrible disease.

How he got the time to meet all these women was a mystery. No wonder money was always short. He must have been spending it all over the place and he ran an expensive motor. He had an E Type Jaguar. I was working harder than ever.

When we bought the new house and installed the nurses as tenants, we decided to throw a party to celebrate. Of course the old lady from the middle floor flat had moved on to live with her sister by then.

A neighbour, who lived around the corner from our other house in Nunhead, worked at Smithfield Meat market. He very kindly got us fabulous joints of meat to roast for it and slice up cold with salads, pickles and French bread. It was a feast, we had a friend in a Chef's hat carving and serving. It all looked very professional. Another friend got us barrels of beer and somehow we obtained loads of other goodies and gorgeous wines etc. The nurses all dressed up in 'Bunny girl' outfits with black fishnet tights and bunny ears. They looked wonderful and the guest list was large. Some said that it was the best party that they had ever been to. I can quite believe it, the music, food and drink were marvellous.

I am afraid that most of the youngsters got 'stoned', in one of the kitchens. That was the age we lived in, what could I do? There were no nasty happenings though, a good time was had by all.

On what turned out to be Guy and my last Christmas, we were all prepared to install my Mother into the new big house, with a granny flat made for her. As soon as the festival was over, we were all set to do the big removal. First we were going to have a nice Christmas at our cottage. Guy went down to Hoo to fetch her. He arrived at Mums' very late with Babs. the Staff Nurse he was sleeping with. I did not know anything about this. They arrived so late to Mother's; it was obvious to her that they had stopped en route.

Mum got to my house not too long before midnight, I had done everything and it looked so lovely, with the tree sparkling and a fire lit. I was upset that he was late getting Mum back to see everything, but believed his story that he had broken down on the way to get her. I saw that Mum was in a rare old temper with him, but assumed that after a night's sleep she would be fine. She didn't tell me what she knew. I guess she didn't want to break my heart, especially at Christmas.

We had reached the point, where Guy found me all unsuspectingly naive and irritating. No matter how carelessly he behaved I saw the best in him. I continued to be loving and thrilled with our life and baby. He saw the houses, as a great asset and earner. He saw me as someone who held him back, he wanted without a conscience, to be able to spend lavishly on his mistresses and I had to go.

I was in the way of his enjoying the proceeds. He was sick of having to think up lies and provide me and my family, with funds and attention. If only I could vanish out of his life for good.

I began to have 'accidents.' I received an almighty shock off the electric kettle in the kitchen. I was thankfully wearing rubber soled slippers. I was usually in bare feet, but there was a wet patch on the kitchen carpet and it felt horrid to walk on. As I was in the middle of something messy, my hands were damp and when I touched the kettle, I got a big shock from it. I suspect now that the wiring was altered in the plug. I was totally freaked out and Guy had to look at it for me and put it right.

On another occasion, he gave me a vehicle with very loose steering. The police stopped me when I was driving over Wandsworth common, on the South Circular and asked me if I had been drinking? The car was wandering all over the road. They should have confiscated it and had it checked. No, when they were certain that I had only been drinking tea, they let me go on. Other times the wheel nuts were loose and the wheels were wobbling.

I still had no idea that they were sabotaged. I just supposed that Guy had trusted my driving ability to such a great extent, he allowed me to use whichever old car that he was in the process of working on next, to sell. I felt flattered. I really didn't imagine that he would try to kill or maim the woman, who was the mother of his gorgeous, four year old son. Not to mention the fact that I was sometimes driving around with him on board.

The worst thing was that he had gone off my oldest son. They no longer spoke very much anymore.

Guy and I had spent a day and evening with Stephanie, her new husband and little daughter, in Surrey. When we arrived back late, the house had been saved by the local Fire Service.

The fire engine was just driving away. The fire had started when my eldest son had been walking his girlfriend to the bus. The large Aztec design cushion had been pushed against the night storage heater, which was in front of the bay window. Guy had turned the heater to 'maximum' for some reason; it caused the cushion to suffer from *internal combustion*.

The Guipure lace curtains went up immediately, followed by the wine coloured velvet ones. Whilst my lad was out, the front window was burning brightly. The elderly lady opposite was taking her little dog out for his evening constitutional. She miraculously looked across and saw it. It was she who had called the Fire service and saved the house. Bless that old lady, there would have been no house very quickly, it was a very old cottage and tinder dry. We had buildings insurance of course, but stupidly we were not insured for contents. I would have lost everything and probably my boy as well, had he not been walking his cute little first girl friend to the bus stop. What a terrible thing to come home to, after a lovely day out.

We had so much cleaning from the smoke damage. It blackened everything. I spent all my spare time washing paint, wood and book spines. Only a few things were lost from the heat. We lost a beautiful wine decanter which was very old and some glasses which were on the tray on top of the bookcase. The carpet was ruined of course from the firemen's boots. It was little enough compared to what life would have been like, had the whole house gone up or if the fire had happened later when we were all sleeping upstairs. I have never stopped thanking my guardian angel or whoever it was, for looking after things. I was saved from disaster so many times.

After that, my son was invited to stay at his girl friend's house in Wandsworth.

When the fire happened, he didn't do his share of cleaning and exited stage left in double quick time. A typical teenager, but Guy criticized him all the time. He was just sixteen and boys of that age are a bit irresponsible. The fire was nothing to do with him however. He had begun to dislike Guy intensely, because he knew things I did not. Guy's attitude to him was no longer so friendly.

Chapter Thirty

I missed my lad and worried about how he would be, so far away. He cycled to his school in Forest Hill and told me that he needed better gears on his bike. I resolved to get them as a surprise, from a shop not far away . . . but did not tell Guy.

I was selling my clothes and varied goods, in several hospitals' foyers. The nurses and doctors loved the things I displayed on my stall and table. Guy would drive the front vehicle with the dress rails and stock in, I would follow on in the car, or whatever we had running at the time. Currently, we were using two ex. post office vans. They had no bonnet and were heavy old things.

The route to the hospital we were selling at that day, took us past the cycle shop. Guy drove off ahead with the youngster and the dress rails. I had the stock in boxes in my van. This was unusual, he usually took the boxes. He drove off to get everything set up. I did one or two things that I had to do at home and then followed. The journey wasn't too far but took me up a large hill and down the other side, it was really steep.

Just over the top of the hill, on the opposite side of the road, was the bike shop. As I drove, the last of the brake fluid drained out of the system. As I topped the hill, I changed down to second gear so that I could slow and cross the road. *To my horror, I had no brakes.* Thankfully, I was in second gear by then. I managed to use the handbrake and being in the low gear, just slowed in time, before hitting the car in front. The way across the road was mercifully clear and there was a space to park. It was a miracle I managed to stop. I went into the cycle shop, my face white and my heart racing. The assistant gave me a drink of water and made me sit down. Had I not been going to that shop, I would have bowled merrily down the hill and tried to turn right at the bottom. I would have slammed into the large brick wall opposite; on the left side of the right hand turn. That is . . . if I hadn't hit a car coming up the other side, before I could turn right. When I recovered, I decided to drive on to the hospital as there were no more drastic hills en route. I simply stayed in second gear and with a hand on the hand brake, took the risk.

When I drove up outside the hospital's foyer, Guy was erecting the rails. I could see him quite plainly looking at me. His face was full of hatred. Somehow I still didn't know that the brakes were deliberately cut. I just couldn't imagine that a man could try to murder someone who had given him such a wonderful son. The victim is often the last to suspect. His look told me that our day was done, love had left.

I was shockingly unhappy that he no longer loved or really wanted me. It was my first husband all over again, the dreadful feeling of no longer mattering to someone. I knew then that it was finished between us. Although I am sure I was meant not to reach that hospital in retrospect, at the time, I did not know what he must have done. So I sold my stock and packed up the remainder into the boxes, afterwards. Then we swapped vehicles and he drove on home. I had our little son with me and I followed.

I could go nowhere, I was alerted though. I felt worried that it was no accident, the more I thought about it. I was chilled, the more I thought about his face when I arrived outside the hospital. Did I tell the police? No I did not. My little son was his, he looked like him. I couldn't bear to think of the implications. I soldiered on, but watching points.

One day a little later, we had to go somewhere together, I forget why. On the way back, he was taking his time. I was sick of being out so long and Matthew needed his tea. He stopped at an antique shop and seemed reluctant to hurry home. There was nothing that I wanted to see there. After my nagging, we went on again slowly. When we reached home, there was a hole in the window and someone was in there. I was scared, 'Be careful Guy' I cried. He said that little Matthew and I should stay safe in the car, while he went in. What happened I did not observe as I was waiting, panicking, in the car. He had obviously, to anyone but me; set this burglary up. The thief was, in retrospect, obviously the son of his girlfriend who lived in the parallel road, behind ours. I discovered later that the lad was taking a Class 'A' drug. He helped the boy into the back garden and over the fence. By then, I was out of the car and running into the house. I didn't see anyone. I ran into the garden and helped Guy support the fence, which no doubt had broken when Guy had assisted the lad over. It was falling inwards. It gouged a chunk out of my arm, I still have the scar.

When we got back inside, the jewellery had been sorted into two piles. The 'dress jewellery' and the real expensive and treasured pieces. Most of those of course, had gone. The dress jewellery, the stuff I had been selling, had the company's name on the back and was lying in a checked out heap. The lad had known what to look for. He also took lots of precious things from out of my glass cabinet as well, the door had been forced. I had Wedgewood and Victorian serving dishes . . . many things that were valuable if you knew a good 'fence.' Most were antiques that I had accumulated and were valuable. Many were treasures that Mum had given to me, it was tragic. I did not suspect Guy for setting this up until later. He was still being nice to me, fooling me and planning my non-existent future.

When people ask me why I did not call the police? I left it all to Guy to handle. He (I thought) loved us, he kept saying so. Because we were broke at that time, I wasn't insured for theft—what folly, I learned a hard lesson. I was terribly occupied with my work, my children and paying the mortgages on the two houses. Mum was poorly and I had to look after her. I was so busy, that I just didn't suspect that anything was directly related to him. If only I had called 999 immediately upon seeing the hole in the front bay window, everything would have become clear, all the fingerprints were gone—if there had been any in the first place, by the time the law turned up. The detection was poor though; there must have been many clues available, especially the entry and the mysterious way that I was kept for so long doing nothing, in the car that day.

I was thinking that things were peculiar; so many things seemed to happen to *US*. It hadn't occurred to me that they were really happening *to me alone*. I did not know he was sleeping with other women. Had I realised that he had others, I would have stopped loving him immediately and been much more on the ball. However, I did not know and even though I wasn't a young girl, I was a very trusting person.

I found that I constantly needed to be comforted by him for the things that went wrong. **He was the cause.**

I really did not realise. He was cunning and evil but, he didn't show hatred in any way, when we were together. He was affectionate to Matthew and me; I think he must have had mental issues. I bet some readers think that I had mental issues too; I was so slow to catch on to the unfolding picture. The real brutality that I couldn't fail to realise was Guy's doing, all came about at the end of our relationship. I had guessed that he was sleeping with the woman who lived in the road behind ours, and hid in the car one dark night to try to catch him emerging from her front door. Suddenly he roared up the road past me coming from another direction completely. He hadn't been at her house at all. I had been sitting there in my car with the window open listening to the night sounds; an autumn leaf bowled along the road caught in the breeze, it was so loud in the complete silence of that lonely street. After he whizzed past me, I drove back around the corner and parked at the front. I went in and asked where the hell he had come from so late? His answer was to punch me on the head with a mighty blow and by his language I could tell that he had been drinking. I ran out to the car, it was raining. The keys were in the kitchen—I had left them on the table. Where could I go for safety, I was too afraid to go back in and get them? I heard him lock the metal porch, keeping me out. I decided to go down the road to a house where a pretty woman had previously held a jewellery party for me, it was getting late by now. I walked in the rain to her house and knocked. She was so surprised to see me standing there, rubbing the lump on my head. I felt so groggy. 'Come in, come in' she said—I stumbled in and burst into tears. Then I told her all that had transpired. She said that I could spend the night on her sofa and go back in the morning. I said that she was very kind and it would suit me very well. First though I needed to be driven to my door and listen, to make sure that Matthew hadn't been disturbed and was crying for me. I had been checking him every five minutes or so whilst I was waiting for Guy to come back. Why the heck hadn't I called the police and had him taken for a night in the cells? I could have shown the lump on my head. Instead I was the one locked out. He had been driving under the influence too. The woman's husband named Bill said that yes, he would drive me round to my door so that I could put my mind at rest. I knew that Guy wouldn't harm little Matthew as he was devoted to him (or so I thought then).

We listened at the door and all was quiet. I got back into his motor to be taken back but he deviated onto Strakers road, a little road that went through the park at Peckham, ending in a dead end. I said what are you doing here? He started undoing his trousers and I knew that I was in mortal danger. I quickly said, 'No Bill, I feel very sick from the blow to the head that Guy gave me'. Then my self-preservation instinct kicked in. I said, 'I didn't know that you fancied me Bill, but we had better wait until later as I would be wrecking your car as I feel very sick.' I pretended that I was grateful saying 'Thanks for the offer but I hope that you will ask me again later'. He said 'You don't know what you are missing Babe'. I said that I was sure it would be wonderful but I wouldn't enjoy however great he was, as I should puke over him and the car. With that—thank god, he turned around and drove back to his house. I pushed a chair up against the door knob and tried to sleep, I was in shock—it had been a near thing. Next morning I declined breakfast and his wife drove me home. The porch was unlocked and Guy was in the kitchen. He never said a word, but I told him what his so called friend had tried to do to me. I asked him to go down and deal with him, but he wouldn't. I said, 'I am the Mother of your son, doesn't that mean anything to you?' He just ignored me. I knew that it was the end but I was to have another dreadful happening before the last day came. The final episodes were within a few days of each other and I was planning my get away from the house.

Up until then, because I had gone short of love and attention in my life, I lived in some sort of dream, only noticing the good bits. I could no longer stay with him; he had no pride or decency. No wonder so many women get murdered by their husbands and lovers. You are always the last to know. Although it may feel bad at the time, it doesn't feel terminal, there is always hope. A union that takes time to evolve needs time to end. It is impossible for the mind to grasp that a person who has made such sweet love to you and provided you with a wonderful child or in the case of many women—children, could have emotionally moved on in such a short time. Do men ever love? Is it just a case of *ownership,* pride of possession? I suppose nature made them to 'flit from flower to flower' like the words in the song from the 'King and I'—that wonderful musical (Mothers' favourite) by Rodgers and Hammerstein. We females grow up believing in Love ever After—I blame the fairy tales. Once that impregnation has taken place, the majority wish to move on to the next available female. Statistically, a few don't. Those men are worth their weight in gold.

If only my mother had told me what she had seen in the first place. She did not want to make waves I suppose. Often the messenger gets it in the neck. She could have been afraid that I would stop looking after her. She took lots of medicines, maybe her judgement was impaired.

Perhaps she was afraid of Guy. He could have warned her to keep quiet, especially about the nurse she knew about. A man with a hidden agenda is dangerous.

Had I called the police and told them about the brakes they would have had the van in for a check and seen the cut brake fluid pipe. However, the minute Guy got that van back, he rectified the fault and the evidence was lost. I constantly lost my chances to get evidence, I was an idiot.

Before the brake incident, I had not felt real dislike from him and certainly not hatred. Even until I had arrived at that hospital's foyer and seen his expression, I had not suspected that the non existent brakes were intentional. We were on borrowed time then, *at last I knew it.* Previously I felt that although things were different between us, we still had a healthy sex life—things were able to be rectified. I suppose that was no effort for him, he was a sex addict. The lovemaking act means so much to a female, I felt cherished at that time. He was lying in his teeth; I might as well have been a knot hole in the fence. I suppose it was imperative that I feared nothing about him, he was still planning. It was afterwards, that so much fitted together like a jigsaw.

Meanwhile, the three of us were still at Nunhead. The other property next door was sufficiently finished for the gay guys to move into.

The two older children had nice rooms at the other house with their Grandma. They lived there or stayed at friend's places, they were independent and as long as they went to their respective schools, I was happy with how they lived. I trusted them.

I always kept in close contact and spent time at the other house with them. Mum took over Corky the cat, he loved her as she smoked and so did he. He must have missed nicotine terribly, when he was given to me. His previous owner smoked cigars and he used to lie on her stomach, getting well kippered. Anyhow, they were all happy and Guy 'appeared' to be proud of me, when I saved a baby from certain death, one afternoon. This is the story.

I had been collecting a shoe bag for my daughter's school, made by my friend around the corner, who sewed. My girl had gym classes and had to hang the shoes on a hook, in the named bag. When walking on the way home, I passed a door out of which cries and moans were emitting.

Sobs and moans and *from a woman*. I took a chance and knocked. A Chinese man came to the door. Are you beating your wife? I asked. "NO" he said. Behind him a Chinese woman appeared, weeping copiously. She nodded 'Yes' and showed me her cheek. There were bruises. The man, our local fish and chip shop owner said, "Come and see this and you'll see why." I took my courage into my two hands and stepped inside. I was shaken to see a little baby of about eighteen months sitting on his potty, covered in blood. He had a swollen and freshly scarred eyebrow and blood from his nose and burn marks all over him. The man said, "She has done that, she hates him." I said that he would soon be dead at this rate, he agreed. He said that his wife had left the baby with *his* mother in Singapore, she loathed her mother-in-law. When she got him back, she hated him.

She had an older daughter who was born in this country; she looked fine and was obviously looked after properly and loved, by the mother. I told him to write the baby's name and age on a piece of paper, with his address. He did as I said. I told him that I had friends at Peckham

Social Services who would help the family out and save him, before she killed him. He said, "They will not take the baby away will they?" I said no, but they would find someone to Foster him in the day. *I knew no one in Social Services*, but I hoped that they would immediately take the baby into hospital and away from her. I ran home and phoned quickly, finding the number from enquiries. The head of the section talked to me, he said "Go back to the house and stay with the little boy." I had become less courageous by then, thinking that the bloke would be thinking of possible recrimination. I said, 'come as quick as you can, I shall wait outside and listen'.

The man and his colleague drove around within ten minutes. They came armed with a clip board. I said 'Put that away, they think that you and I are friends, they will not speak if you look official.' "Good point" said the woman. We knocked and I introduced them as my friends. When the man went up to the baby's bedroom with the father, the little chap was in his cot. He gasped when he saw him and so did his colleague when he carried him down all wrapped up in a blanket. He looked so still and so pathetic. He hadn't got long to survive, had he stayed there.

I went out at this point. They dialled 999 straight away, the police and ambulance came and the mother and baby were taken away. I removed myself from the spot, double quick. I had a little one to protect also. I did not want revenge taken against me later.

The baby went straight off to hospital. They promised to let me know what happened. Later that week they called by phone and thanked me. It was enough. If only I had used that fish and chip shop, I may have seen the little boy showing distress much earlier, I didn't like the look of it though so never went in.

Strangely, I was able to find out what happened to the child, from my plasterer who was a friend. I was having work done to the hall ceiling at the other house where I was now living, having recently left Guy. The plasterer's girlfriend was a nurse on the admission ward that night. He told me that the baby was terribly poorly. She had been burning him with cigarettes all over his little body. The pain he must have suffered. I began to wish that the husband had hit her harder. I was told that she was sentenced to prison, but she must have been *unhinged* to have done that. What happened to any of them later on, I never knew. It had all occurred just before the event that finally made me leave Guy and our little house at Nunhead.

Chapter Thirty One

I had been holding a jewellery party in someone's house and I finished rather early. Upon returning home, I found the house deserted and my four year olds little bed empty—where was he? I looked in the workshop and there on a clip board, was a photo of a woman we both knew who lived in Penge. She had been a secretary to the Removal firm that Guy had been working for, maintaining the Removal Lorries. The owner had been a close friend of Guys. I was puzzled, why was a photograph of his secretary sitting on Guy's clip board? I decided to drive over to Penge to see her. I knew well where she lived; she and I had spoken on a few occasions. I knew that she liked men. She once had told me that she had three men on the go at the same time. I said 'Oh well, I have enough trouble with just one.' *Little did I know that one of them was Guy.* When I rang her door bell, they were both in there and my child was fast asleep on the sofa in the other room. I was **shocked**. They were looking at photographs and drinking Bacardi and Cokes. I said, 'What are you doing here Guy?' He said, 'Mind your own business, you can't pull my strings, I am not your puppet.' I looked at the woman, 'Are you two having an affair?' As she said 'Yes' Guy said 'No.'

I knew then, that they were. He looked shifty and she was gloating. I said to Guy, that as we were not actually

168

married, he should behave even more loyally. He owed it to me.

He told me to 'F—off.'

I felt like a humiliated **Nothing**. Full of fury, I flung the nearest ashtray at Guy, it was a heavy one. It connected. A cut appeared over his eye. 'Look what you have done to him' she cried, full of concern. I saw 'double' red. I went to clout her with my handbag—that was the last thing I can remember. I was punched to the floor. They took out their hate on me with their feet, by the state of my body when I eventually came around. It was hard to breathe and their kicking caused my spine to be dislocated. I was unconscious for some time. It was amazing that I managed to get up and walk but I was staggering. I tottered into the other room and got my little one from the sofa with his blue Star Wars 'picky' blanket, all picked to death and very comforting. I managed to walk outside with him tucked against me. My shoes had come off. I left them, but managed to take my bag and keys. I got the little one in to my old Renault 4. The old car was fortunately quite high off the ground and easy to drive, with the gearstick on the dashboard, instead of the floor, it also had a bench seat. It had a nice soft clutch and I was able to drive it safely.

I tore away to get us help from my Mother and my daughter at Herne Hill, my eldest son being at friends. I dared not go to the cottage.

I sat outside. It was midnight by now, the place was deserted.

As luck would have it, my next door neighbours had been dining out. They were a young couple. He was an actor and she an anaesthetist at Kings. They lived together and whenever I see him now in a film, I remember that night. They helped get the little one in and Mum got him to bed. They then took me down to the hospital. Alas, that very night a man got himself stabbed in a drunken brawl and I got short shrift. My tummy was cursorily felt and I was pronounced fine to go. They missed the spine altogether. I went back to my Mothers' and was helped onto a spare bed.

All was quiet that night. I cried a lot before I managed to sleep, I was in a lot of pain too. Mum and my daughter took it in turns to stay awake, just in case. All was quiet. Again I didn't call the police. The next day, I was black and blue. My spine was in agony and my left leg wouldn't walk properly. I managed to get myself to my doctors at Nunhead, it was hard to drive but I managed because I couldn't bear the alternative and the hospital hadn't been much good.

When I told my doctor what had happened, he felt my back and soon figured out what was wrong. He put his knee against a little cushion which he held on my spine, pushed and in a trice the bones were in the right place again. Magic . . . I could walk properly and the sciatic nerve was released. All the pain gradually drifted away. He noted the bruises and checked my ribs and sent me away with pain killers.

I was never to go and live in the cottage again. It was an unlucky little house. Thinking what had happened to the previous owner, I was glad to be gone from there. A day or two later, when Guy was out somewhere, I let myself in to get clothes and the things I needed. I took very little as I had to get out of there fast.

My young teenage daughter, although knowing my suffering at Guy's hands, still imagined that he would be reasonable with her. He had at first, been very lovely to the children. He provided Nicola with a 50cc 'step through' Honda motor cycle, when she was old enough. He maintained it for her and taught her to ride it. I think that at that difficult age, she imagined that her Mum couldn't have been entirely saintly. *She herself was the usual teenager, irritated by me at the least little thing.* She inferred that it was probably six of one, and half a dozen of the other. I didn't have to point out to her, how very *incorrect* she was.

She rode around to him to make adjustments to the bike. After doing them, he said to her 'Tell your mother not to come round to the cottage snooping, if she does, we will kill her and put her into one of the old graves in the cemetery.' She jumped onto her little motor bike and sped off. Thinking that I might be about to leave the other house and go around to collect something again from the cottage, she stopped at the call box in Dulwich village and phoned me. I heard a hysterical voice begging me not to go there and telling me between sobs, all he had said. Poor little girl, imagine saying such a cruel thing to a kid. What a *gross* pig, (that insults pigs, who are lovely intelligent creatures, which is more than can be said about him). Actually it did me a huge favour. I think that from that moment on, she understood much more. I no longer felt that I had to *justify* anything.

Guy first came around with an axe and threatened me from the pavement outside. I had changed the locks and the tenants all exited stage left. I called 999 and the Streatham Police drove down straight away. Guy drove off quickly. They said that they would drive past on and off, to check that we were alright. We got sick of having no decent sleep, I was too scared. In those days, the police tended to regard such happenings as being a 'domestic' and they did not interfere. That is one thing that has improved thank goodness. They have no time for 'batterers' now and instigate proceedings in case the woman is too scared. WHICH I WAS—I was terrified that our house would be burned down.

The next visit from Guy, resulted in him chopping the phone off from outside, so that I could *not* call the police. Next door's phone was cut off as well, which made them furious. They both would have desperately needed it for their respective jobs. I had to do something.

One of the girls that had stayed at the house came back. She was plucky. I had really liked her as a tenant. She had a bloke who was tall and good looking, hanging around after her, but she wasn't interested. I got to chatting to him in our kitchen one afternoon, he suggested that he should have a room at my place and be my bodyguard. I had a smallish, but ideal room and said I would charge him no rent. Unfortunately, I *couldn't* afford wages.

He said that being under the same roof as the girl he hankered after, would be enough. He was six feet two inches and had hands like hams and was athletic and powerful. I really liked him and wished that I was ten years younger. He was fantastic to have as a friend and adored my little one. He used to 'zoom' him around the house playing 'Superman', his feet thundering on the stairs. My toddler loved being held out in front, his little arms pointing ahead, playing flying—they were *both* like kids.

He was sweet to the whole family. He couldn't interest my tenant though. Sadly, she was a lesbian—poor Steve. She had a nice girl friend. Steve had a great following from nurses and there were always lovely girls having a cup of tea in my kitchen. You always want what you can't have so, I am told.

I was getting over Guy fast. The lack of stress was great. He had stopped coming around threatening me. Steve had been to see him at my instigation. He warned Guy that if he approached any member of my family in any way, or threatened us, he would put some people he knew in the East End, on to him. It certainly worked. One evening, Steve and I went off to a party in the East End. Steve introduced me to a skinny, weedy fellow named Willie. This Willie was a 'Hit man' according to Steve and had offered to 'vanish' Guy for free. I felt very scared, what on earth was I doing at a party with the likes of him? I had to be very polite and say 'No thanks, but thanks for the offer' when all I wanted to do was scream. There are some awful types in London just looking for mischief. How on earth could I have ever looked at my darling little son again if I had done such a thing to his father? Guy may have wanted to 'vanish' me, but two wrongs don't make a right. My son had his daddy's features far more than mine. I simply could not have lived with myself and would probably have gone off to Holloway prison as I would have been the prime suspect anyway.

Guy stayed at Nunhead; continuing his liaison with the female who had the little girl, the 'druggie' son and the big dog. They lived locally and he moved in with them. He continued to operate his car business from the rear of our cottage.

He made sure that he didn't send any mail on to me however. The bills were all in my name, because I lived there long before he did. He paid nothing of course. Debts I incurred from the energy services etc. were in the red and court was threatened. With all that was going on, I forgot to notify the relevant offices that I had gone from that address.

173

Eventually, he let the place to an Irish girl, who realised what he was doing and made it her business to find me and let me know. She was a very nice person, but she loathed him, he was dealing with her wrongly as a landlord. She wasn't as green as me and knew her way around life. She told me what to do, so I contacted the companies and they were very understanding. I did not have to go to court, disappointing Guy, no doubt.

He was so completely wicked to me. It was as though I had done something evil to *him*. All I had done was to foolishly love him and work hard for the future of our family.

He certainly gave us no money. He seemed totally uninterested in his child, which surprised me. I was glad. I would have had a difficult time undoing the bad things that he would have taught him. I think he at last cottoned on to the fact, that I could have put him in jail for a long time, for the assault with the secretary. The damage to my spine was witnessed and noted by my doctor. I was desperately bruised also.

I later found out that he had another son from his first wife called Nigel, he ignored him too. He had broken his first wife's jaw. He was a monster and I thought he was wonderful. When you find initial kindness from a man after having a bad time, you fail to look too deeply into his past. You often take them at face value, a big mistake.

After several friendships with men, I still couldn't get it right. I must always go for a certain type of person. These relationships were easily terminated with minimum hassle though, as soon as I saw that they were wrong. Now I am happily alone. I miss the companionship and cuddles but not the danger. I cannot choose right, either they get hacked off with me, or I with them.

In the past I did seem to find strays, usually with a drink problem. I guess I have a lot of 'mothering instinct.' I always imagined that I could improve them, with a lot of love and a happy home life. I now realise that although they improve in the short term, they always slip back into their habits, whether alcohol or women. I obviously have a faulty radar system when it comes to men. Strikes me, it is better to stick to horses and other animals, to indulge my *feelings and attention upon.* They don't dish out pain, apart from when they die and that is pain of a different kind.

I always thought that Guy was a Sociopath. He cared so much for some things, blind people and unfortunates. He just had no conscience. When he got tired of something, he needed it to disappear. He seemed too afraid to do his own violence though, he was cowardly. That was a very good thing in retrospect. I might have been killed off in a fit of rage, *if he had had the guts.*

He brought in a man to sort that side out, before I left our home. A hit man, but a very stupid one. His name was Rob. Guy invited him into our garage to work, ostensibly to make sash windows. Rob lacked a neck; he seemed all shoulder and muscle. He resembled a giant bear, but a bear would have had more brain.

To demonstrate what type he was, not long after leaving the cottage; I again needed something urgently for the little one. I had to go back to the cottage on my own. Guy and Rob were there. They were both working in the garage. I did not go through to it, before I let myself into the kitchen.

Rob's wife was in there making tea, for the two men. He had been bringing his wife round to our house. She was a cowed, skinny little thing. I remembered that when I still lived there, she had come around one afternoon to try to interest me in a piece of lovely jewellery. She said it was from her dead Grandmother. I doubted that, frankly it looked too classy. It was a single row of real pearls with a tigers eye clasp, set with diamonds. I liked it but thought it may have been stolen. I could have been 'set up' as a receiver. I said 'No' and hoped that she would not bring any other ill gotten gains. I had already lost a lovely ruby ring which I normally always wore. It was an heirloom. I had last seen it on the shelf where I had laid it, before I put my fingers into some pastry I was making. I was going to put it back on later. I searched everywhere for it, it was gone.

When I saw her in my kitchen—even though I was living at the other house, I was wild. She looked so at ease in my house. I got angry and told her to get out. I said that I had already lost a ring. Big mistake. In a rage, I stupidly went through to the garage. I was seething. My uncontrollable temper could have got me killed. I was about to shout at Guy, when Rob's wife told her husband what I had said about the ring, thereby accusing her. Rob rushed at me like a Rugby player intercepting the ball. He caught me as I was trying to escape across the lawn. Head down, he shouldered me to the floor with a mighty push. My back went 'ping' again, it was dislocated like before. Thankfully he didn't hit me. I staggered to the house grabbing my keys and drove to the doctor's surgery. He was still in Nunhead; I hadn't re-located to one nearer my other house. He fixed my dislocation again and said that he hoped I could find Peace. I knew that there would be no peace with that *fiend* around our property. I shouldn't go there again.

I wonder if Guy had taken the ring to make me accuse Rob's wife. Maybe Guy had just stolen it, to help fund his other women? I found out later that he was a dreadful thief.

Guy told me that Rob had killed a man, an Asian. He had crawled through a loft to steal and killed a man, in the house. I did not believe it. I assumed he was trying to scare me. Could it have been true?

I also found out that the taxi that Rob was driving was 'Ringed.' A term used by the police for vehicles that were adapted from other newer stolen ones, to an older one, which had the appropriate paperwork with it. Again I could say nothing. I would have come to a nasty end if I had 'Grassed'. *A criminal term which means exposing bad people to the law.*

Guy obviously knew some bad people, men *and* women. I couldn't fit in with his new found occupation; I was *so* in the way. He had to get rid of me.

I eventually returned to the cottage with five muscled young men, who dug the local graves. I had to get my furniture and other belongings. I had another close encounter with Rob. That one was the last, but it nearly ended my life. I was *never to be* closer to death.

Chapter Thirty Two

I had hired a four and a half tonne van for the removal, it was a new Mercedes. My licence entitled me to drive such a vehicle in those days. It came from Balham, not too far away, a few miles. They were scary miles though. I found the width so terrifying. I had never driven a huge vehicle before and this one was colossal.

I cautiously drove the miles over to the cottage, met up with the boys and proceeded to clear out the house. We were getting on famously. I was standing on the ladder checking that I had got everything out of the loft, when suddenly a pair of hands grabbed me around the ankles. It was Guy—someone had called him. He pulled me down the ladder roughly, my chin bumping on the rungs. I was frightened. I called out to the boys but they had gone. Whatever had he threatened them with, that they would desert me like that? He proceeded to drag me by the hair from room to room screaming at me, I couldn't make out what he was saying, he was hysterical. Thank heavens he didn't throw me out of the upstairs window, it was open.

It was fortunate that he was a coward and wouldn't risk his own neck.

He pulled me down the stairs and held me against the back door whilst phoning Rob. The phone was on the wall at the side of the door. He said, 'Rob is coming round to kill you and you are going under one of the old opened graves, in the cemetery'.

At that time, it was a Nature Reserve; people were not being buried there anymore. Many of the graves had been opened by local youths and some decaying old bodies were visible. One fetched up in the front seat of someone's car. It must have been an awful shock. There was no 'reverence' in Nunhead . . .

At that moment, I felt Guy's words were a real probability. I had a weird feeling in my bowels. I was held with my back against the door, his arm across my neck.

I heard the taxi engine in the distance. 'Here he comes' said Guy with a sadistic look on his face. With that, I took an almighty bite out of his arm, sinking my teeth right into it. I had a mouthful of blood, it was horrible but it saved me. He screamed and released me. As he jumped back, I dodged past him, got through the door and made for the truck. Miraculously, Guy had closed the back up and the keys were left in the ignition. I leapt in and started it up. As Rob drove around the corner I whizzed past him, driving hell for leather. I heard Guy shout '*We'll get her the other end*'.

I did not dare go to the other house. I drove (without worrying about the width for one minute) straight to Camberwell Police Station car park.

In those days, there were no gate restrictions and I shot straight in. Hysterically, I fell into the arms of two young Bobby's. Would you believe it, that bastard Rob had followed me into the car park also . . .

The police questioned why he was there? He said "That truck is containing my friend's furniture and she's stealing it," pointing to me. I exclaimed, '**No**, it's all mine and I'm escaping from that man who is after me.' The young Police looked perplexed. I quickly said, 'Ask him what colour diesel is in his tank?' *He had been helping* *himself to red diesel from building sites.* With that, he jumped into his taxi and drove away.

I could breathe again. A detective was fetched and took me into a room. He sat me down with a cup of tea. "I want to hear all of it" he said. I explained that Guy had threatened my life, how I had escaped and that I was only collecting my own household goods. I told most of the story. I was afraid to tell all that I had found out about the stealing, in case Guy had my house in Herne Hill burnt down. I did tell him though, how Guy had obtained a blue, open backed lorry with a view to organising a robbery, (he revealed that to me, after he had been drinking)—I was disgusted.

I would have liked to have known more, so that I could tell the detective. Guy and cronies must have thought I had, because the '*cat was amongst the pigeons*' well and truly. They must have assumed I knew much more than I did. It was revealed over the phone by Guy (in a hurt voice), that it took a long time and a lot of people, to hide their wrong doings. Fancy being as stupid as to reveal that to me. I dare say there were possibly a lot of stolen goods in the garage. There could even have been cars, I didn't know. I did see some old Jags with wire wheels; I just assumed that Guy was collecting them for future sale. I had not been into the garages for a long time, especially since the advent of Rob. I didn't get past the workshop with Guy's cups of tea, my own vehicle being always parked at the front of the house.

The police should have swooped. They could have possibly broken a car 'Ringing' gang. Instead, the CID man told me to stay clear of the place, as he wanted to 'Plot' them. He asked me if I had heard any criminal sayings like 'Blag' used around me. I think he had watched too many television films. I certainly would have told him if I had, but I think that Guy knew that I was not the *'gangster's moll'* type. I wouldn't have countenanced any such thing. Being 'Thick' though, he was very loose mouthed. He could never have made a serious criminal; he would have given all the secrets away at the least provocation. He was always a 'petty' thief, stealing from those who loved him was more his sort of thing.

I felt in retrospect, that the police left it all a bit too late. Had they gone immediately, they possibly could have caught them red handed. I think that it was a real 'den of thieves' even Rob's house had probably got lots of stolen gear in it. Those policemen should have had more sense. They didn't even ask me about him or where he lived. The two Bobby's who saw him drive into the car park in his taxi, should have said something about that—I was too shell shocked at the time.

I was too shocked from my *near death experience* to even talk about him. I expect everything had to be signed in triplicate and mulled over, before the law could do a thing. It was not much better in those days than, we are told it is now, paperwork galore.

I have since realised, why Guy put me through all that long and difficult time, waiting to be able to buy that *particular* cottage. Suffering living in the 'Bread van' and all the other horrors that I went through—the cottage was ideal for nefarious doings. It was not in an overlooked spot and that road was very quiet. I could have found a much larger and more suitable place, if only I had realised. He wanted it for what was around the back, not the accommodation, that wasn't really important.

Talking about the law as it was in the past. I well remember some fifty years ago, seeing my ex. brother in law's private office at his house. He had retired then but had worked for MI 6 and the Port Authority. He had drawers stuffed full with watches and contraband. He must have confiscated them when working for the Port Authority. I saw them, they were new and many. No wonder he was so wealthy and had so many houses. Where there is money, there is corruption. He got cancer and died, but he had a good life before that. I remember him going to boxing matches with other high ranking retired officers. I wonder if they were all in it, up to their necks, also.

To resume my tale . . . I had survived the night thankfully and returned home after hiding the van in a friend's shrubbery filled drive in Dulwich village. I took a cab the next morning back to the hidden van and drove the van over to my house for unloading.

I had to be quick, each extra day I had the van, the hire contract carried a stiff penalty charge. There we were, Mum, my girl, my little fellow and me. I had no masculine help and a full vehicle. I was also watching for Guy, *at that point I didn't have my 'Body-guard.'*

Chapter Thirty Three

A few yards down the road, the Tuning Centre was run by a hard working man and a couple of assistants. He did good work and was always busy. Outside, sitting on the wall, was a blond man waiting for his sports car to be finished. He was watching us. After a while he came up to me. He said, "Excuse me, my name is Joe. I hope you don't think that I am being nosy, but how come you have got to unload that huge van, without anyone to help you?" I explained briefly and he immediately made a phone call on his mobile.

Within a short time, a group of men arrived and he introduced me to them. He said that he was the boss of 'Voids'. *They prepared the council flats for re-letting, when the time came.*

I was stunned to see the men start taking the things into the house and he said that I should direct them with the furniture, to the correct locations. I was very happy and grateful. In no time flat, the entire van was emptied. This young man, walked around my old house, noting cracked windows, broken sashes and missing light fittings. He wrote it all down and promised me that they could fix them. My mouth hung open, I couldn't believe my luck.

He told me to get the removal van back and collect my motor. I hurried the van back and didn't have to pay extra.

What a blessing this was as I had lost all my stock. I had lost my power to earn. Guy had hidden the van with the rails and boxes in it. He said 'What Van?' when I asked for it back. I needed to earn money for my family. I also owed four thousand pounds to Bob at the Warehouse. That was the amount Bob had let me build my credit debt to. True I was selling a lot each week, but now I couldn't pay him back, I had nothing to sell. I was totally broke.

Again my luck held, I screwed up my courage and went to see him. I explained what had been done to me. I told him about the violence. The fear I felt, that my house could be burnt with us in it. He was very sympathetic. He told me not to worry about the debt and to repay it, if I ever came into money.

All I know is; that I was able to give a home to his brother later, when he was in need. It wasn't for very long, but I made a difference to the family and was glad to do it. Not all men are wicked in this world, even though I may give the impression that I think they are. Once again, fate dealt me a hand that was superb.

After I returned in my car from taking the van back, Joe said that I should get my Mum and the children and he would take us around to the local pub for lunch.

We sat in the pub garden and watched the fountain and had pies and chips. *It was the most memorable meal I have ever had in my life.* All my misery and fear was sorted, in the short term. He then took me with him to learn 'Clay shooting' at the local shooting club.

I purchased a Baikal 'under and over' shotgun. I had the police come around and make things legal and got a license. I didn't need to put in cartridges. Guy would never know that it was empty. When he next came round with his axe, I pointed it out of the window at him. He said "Is that a gun?" I replied 'Yes and I'll blow you to hell, if you come in here.' He spat on the pavement and went away. The situation was sorted, no more chopping off the phone and embarrassing me with the lovely people next door. No more threats of what he would do to us.

Forty years ago, when I was so vulnerable with an elderly Mum with cancer and three young children, it seemed the only way *and it worked.* Joe had rescued me from a horrendous situation and I started going out with him. He was single and divorced and so was I. We got on very well and he was so kind to us. Mother adored him.

After some period of time being my right hand man, teaching my little one to ride a bike, plus extensive knowledge of computers. He met a lady who he had known, when he was young. He fell in love with her and made me sad because, I knew that we were through. We would have to manage, minus Joe. Joe had an incredibly high I.Q. His was so high that it was rare. They say genius and madness are very close; he was eventually to change into someone none of us could recognise.

Alas, he went into a world of mental aberration . . . he kept many guns and was cruel to the woman he replaced me for. He had married her by then and they had their own baby girl, as well as her four boys from a previous marriage. He had a mental breakdown and he tortured them. *He had suffered one in his teens apparently.* I was out of the relationship and very lucky to be so, in the end. He became completely crazy and was put into prison. It should have been a mental facility I think, that would have been the correct place. The things he did. He was never sane.

It was very sad for my little one though, once again he lost a father figure. Mum and I too, lost a friend.

My 'Bodyguard' had fallen in love and gone off with a woman by then, we missed him.

The older Children closed ranks. They protected and gave a lot of love and attention to their little brother.

I remember going back in time, just after we had escaped from Guy, how Mum and I had cried one day. He was standing with his thumb in, swaying to the song 'Daddy's Home' by Cliff Richard, as it played on Mum's turn table. He kept putting it on and breaking our hearts, he was remembering his daddy. What could we do? He was bed wetting and stuttering. The loss was taking a terrible toll on him. Isn't it sad that it is the children who always suffer the most; they are too young to understand? Guy no longer wanted him. As time went by, he gradually forgot and with Steve playing with him around the house, he thought less and less about his father. The stuttering and bed wetting eventually ceased and I knew he was on the mend.

I got a new Siamese kitten for him. We called him 'Willy Wonka' and he adored him. With a loving Grandma on hand, the two pets and his big brother and sister, he seemed to recover well and become happy again. He was so absorbed with computers and building them. He was very sophisticated for one so young, his knowledge was amazing. We ALL began to become happy again.

I had several adventures living at Herne Hill. One was very upsetting.

Chapter Thirty Four

I used to observe from my upstairs kitchen window, a little boy of about nine years old. He was out in all weathers on his bike. He never seemed to go in until it got dark.

I stopped him one day and asked him where he lived. He told me that his name was Paul and said that his Mum went past, walking to the shops to get shopping. He said that he would point her out to me. Sure enough, his Mum came past as Paul and I were speaking and I stopped her, to chat.

She told me a shocking tale about the man she had married. He seemed a charming, kind and generous person, when she met him at the bar where she worked. They started going out together and he liked Paul, her little boy. Eventually they married and she moved into his big house in my road.

At first he was appreciative of her efforts to keep the place immaculate, the garden was the same. She had planted roses; it looked beautiful. She was so proud of it and after a coffee with me, at my place; she took me to see it. Her husband was out. It was true, it was lovely. She said, there was just one problem, he had turned against her and was hitting her and wouldn't let Paul into the house. I was horrified. The little lad was terrified and wetting the bed.

On his mantelshelf was an Urn, the type that one would get from a Crematorium. She told me that his first wife's ashes were in there. He constantly threatened that hers would make a matching pair. *He was a London Gangster and his daily life was criminal.* My goodness, you did not have to look far in London, to find bad men. I began to think better of Malvern, why had I ever left?

It was obvious that she was very unsafe and when she showed me the array of sawn off shotguns in a chest in the sitting room, I realised I was too. I had better get out of there quick.

I let the little fellow into my house whenever rain came, he knew to knock.

If her husband came back unexpectedly, the story was to be, that he was playing with my son. I plotted to remove her from there. I went to the child's school and told the headmistress everything. She was very concerned and understanding. I promised that I would do my best. She said that Paul had been a happy little boy at first. Now he was a nervous wreck. I researched and found a shelter for women in North London. I phoned them and they said to bring them both as soon as I could, a place would be found for them. I had to work on my new found friend.

She was terrified and had not had long enough really, to stop loving the man, who had once been so good to them.

It takes quite a while to *lose* love. I remember begging Guy to hold my hand once, when I knew he had gone off me. He took pleasure in refusing. It isn't easy, as I well knew. This would sound odd to all those, who have not suddenly been *turned upon* by someone who loved them. How can you not hate *instantly*, when your child is suffering like that? It is strange that as love takes a time to grow, it also takes a time to switch off. I also knew this, first hand.

I had a bit of a battle with her; to explain, that he would never revert back to the other person she had known and fallen for.

If she wasn't very careful, *she* was destined for the mantelshelf. *Then, what would happen to her son?*

One morning, after she had gathered together his best toy and their change of clothes, stuffed them into a couple of carrier bags, leaving much to his chagrin, his new little bike. I put them both into my car and drove them away.

The old Irishman upstairs in the little flat, kept our secret because he liked them both and would miss them. Nothing must come back to me. I could be killed for doing this. It was a fair old drive and the refuge was a bit tough, but there was peace of mind there.

She promised to make a new life and thanked me profusely. I didn't need thanking; I just looked at the face of her little boy.

A while later when I was working in the front garden clipping the hedge, her husband drew up in his car. He got out and questioned me. Did I know her? I said 'Yes, vaguely.' I told him that I knew her little boy who spoke to mine, sometimes. Did I know where she had gone? I said no, I hadn't realised that they *had* gone. He seemed to believe me, thank heavens. He didn't bother me again. The little Irishman winked at me one day when he passed, as I was parking. I know I saved her life. You need an *ally* to do some things in life that take courage and they certainly had me.

Before I recounted this memory, I was telling you about the stage I was in, concerning the 'split' from Guy.

Now was the time to start building a future. The next stage was to sell up. Divide the assets and re-start our lives. Guy and I would both have been well off.

I sent the manager of the building society, my friend, around with a note suggesting this. I said in it, that the only winners if we went to law would be the solicitors. I said in the note that we need not see each other, as we could each use a representative. Guy, ever brainless, informed him that if he ever saw me, he would kill me. He was an idiot.

I felt embarrassed to ever have loved such a fool.

Even the Bank Manager from my local bank in Tulse Hill, where we had a joint account, came over to warn me that he was threatening my life. Guy was making stupid pathetic threats because he was beaten. He refused to amicably settle things and he would have had a settlement of the three houses, instead of just two. I was to give him a severe trouncing in the High Court later.

My solicitor was a sweet woman, she and I got on just fine. She used to teach piano before taking up Law. She advised me well, but must have done something that her firm didn't like, because she was to go back to teaching. What a loss she was.

My case was taken over by the Senior Partner and my costs escalated. Eventually the company moved to the city and my costs trebled.

I spent years living badly, because things dragged on so much. Guy used delaying tactics. He was doubtless acquiring more property with his woman. I know she sold up and they bought a house in Dulwich village. That could not have been cheap. I doubt if it was jointly owned though. I meanwhile, managed the best I could and nursed my Mother, who was getting much worse by then.

I could give a blow by blow account of how things went with the solicitors, they were difficult. You would get bored. I will just say that Guy made out that the occupants of the houses were just 'care-taking' no rent being paid. I went through the dustbins one dark night and put filled black bags of my own in them, so that I could take away the rubbish for inspection. I put their stuff on the top so that it all looked as normal, *but what I discovered inside* . . . It was an Aladdin's Cave. The proof that the occupiers were on Housing Benefit and getting rent paid, was screwed up inside and a page of practised signatures was in the other black bag, in the other bin. The female friend of Guy's was practising signing like him, what was she up to? I was intrigued and my solicitor (at that time it was the girl I liked) said that I should have been a private investigator. We now had the very total of monies paid to the occupants. My solicitor wrote to the department and found how much, for proof in court and we were able to know the exact amounts. The gay chaps had gone and Guy had installed a prostitute. Guy of course, was now residing in Dulwich village with his lady friend.

He certainly was being un-cooperative, he delayed everything he could. Events also *stayed my hand* a bit. I had them full with Mother.

She had become very frail and my girl came over from Australia where she was then living, to spend Christmas and help me look after her. She also came to court with me when my firm of solicitors got court dates arranged.

As you can imagine, things were grim for me. Mum was ill with pneumonia as well. She had been visited by a friend of hers. The woman had a cold. Mum's immune system being low, she caught it. We had a MacMillan nurse who helped us, they are wonderful. My poor Mother passed away and we were shattered.

She had a life of being looked after by me and not in a hospital ward or a Hospice. Mum specifically wanted to remain at home. She was able to see her little grandson until the end.

My darling daughter helped me, she also came to the High Court with me as I mentioned, when my case resumed and gave me confidence there as well.

When my case was eventually prepared, I had a Barrister. He was a super fellow, handsome and nice, he was recently married. Alas he was eventually to die from Asbestosis. So sad, that old building material, used so often in sheds and many other things, kills frequently. It is handled with care now, but then, people simply did not realise how lethal it was.

My replacement Barrister was a man with complexities in his personality. He did not seem keen on me but he was nevertheless a super helper for the judge (called The Master). He re-arranged his bag for him and was helpful for the poor chap, who had to hear a lot of horrid stuff about my treatment.

During the period of the case, I had two Barristers, several solicitors and three different Masters.

At the end I was apologised to by Master Gowers, the final judge. He said that he wished it had not have had to have taken so long and put me in such a difficult position with my circumstances. He was obviously really so sorry for me and he said that Guy was a scoundrel. I smiled at that, I had a word for him that began with 'B' and had seven letters. The Master was a lovely man with a kind face, who wanted to hear all the detail about my mistreatment, apart from the statement which of course, he had read. I think that he may have 'dined out' on me at the end. I wrote a letter to him which my solicitor slated me for. Stupid chap. I think that they must have little thanks for their difficult task of sorting the liars from the truthful.

My girl and I turned many heads at the high court—we brightened up some days in that sombre building. We received compliments too and although it was very serious, it was interesting. The stress and circumstances had made me lose four stone and I looked very nice in my little suits. I had been eleven stone. Fear, loss, stress and grief certainly strip the weight off. I regained so much more energy which helped my life enormously. It must have made Guy do a double take also, I looked like I used to before I had that 'late baby'—losing weight is so hard when you gain it at thirty eight. Guy was always very good at slimming when he put a bit on, he of course was to be seen in the nude by loads of women, no wonder he was trim and sexy to look at. Think of the exercise he was getting unbeknown by me—while I was anchored to my stall selling clothes etc. My Mum always said that getting podgy put most men off women; she was right about so many things. They say stress causes weight gain, I can quite believe it—I was a living example. In the final outcome after days of appearing at the high court in the Strand however, I regained my confidence and belief in myself, I wasn't a failure as a person—unattractive and just a work machine who provided for a family and looked after a sick Mum and wasn't worthy of love. I had become younger looking as the years slipped off me with the peace of mind that I obtained (not to mention the security and financial means).

Yet even then, seeing Guy and the wreck that he had become made me feel sad. He was pathetic and a liar and as I looked years younger, he looked years older. I had to be reminded by my girl that he had tried to murder me more than once and not be so soft hearted. The master called him a villain at the very end of the case and awarded me the house at Herne Hill outright; it was in my name alone and we all lived there, after all. He decreed that Guy, be responsible for the court costs.

If Guy had agreed to the sale and half the proceeds, on the day my pal went to see him on my behalf, he would have been a wealthy man. I felt ashamed that such a low and brainless fellow had given me a son, what on earth did everyone think of my lack of judgement? Having suffered so much in my marriage, I was susceptible for love from any half decent man—I truly thought him fantastic. Anyway, he fooled many other well brought up women, not just me. He was witty and strong and capable, certainly not dreadful at first in our relationship, I thought him brave and kind initially and in my mind I made him the man that I would want, not the man he really was. Or maybe if he hadn't had the selfish dreadful parents that he did have, he could have been a decent human being and not damaged so many people. Or maybe he was mentally 'off centre' in the first place and just a human walking time bomb. These people exist and look normal and seem normal until something makes them change completely. Life is very risky isn't it. It is best to get to know someone for a hell of a long time before throwing your lot in with them . . . let the first glamour go from your eyes before you become permanently attached.

The female who obtained the house in Dulwich village with him, must have put it in her name alone. She dropped him out, as soon as she realised that she wasn't going to get any of my money.

He turned up in court afterwards with a new woman, who was classed as a legal assistant to him. She owned a 'Second Hand' shop and someone who knew her, told me that she worshipped money. I thought that was appropriate, she wasn't so much as a 'second hand rose' she was a multiple hand one . . . How long they lasted together, I never knew.

The court costs, *the legal aid,* had to be repaid. It must have been a vast amount, because although Guy had to pay it, he ran out of funds and I made up the shortfall. That amount was colossal.

Guy ended up getting NOTHING. I got enough for a house outright, my financial troubles were over. If only my Mum had lived to see the day. At least I was able to tell my sister on the phone in Calgary, where she lived—I had someone of my generation to boast to.

We had made up our rift by then, I didn't care for her husband who had made a pass at me and eventually left her for another woman when she was in her late fifties. He left her when her chances of finding love and happiness were limited, as she wasn't working or socially involved with many people. She didn't want to look anyway, she loved him too dearly.

When I criticized him she was cross with me, she couldn't handle any other person even a sister, telling her that he was a bad man. He was a very bad man because he took all her money as well as getting her to sell their big house whilst they (his words) looked for a smaller one as the children were grown. He craftily used that time to hide the cash and vanish with the blond 'younger model' next door. She was a sitting duck being gullible like me; she too had grown up in a refined bubble in the country, never suspecting that there was danger out there. I really thought that once you were married, you would be safe and looked after. All girls should be taught that real life isn't like a fairy tale, the handsome prince sometimes (usually) moves on to fresh fields—generally younger ones. My dear sister has passed away now, I miss her terribly. I must tell you a lovely story about her, to bring the mood back to happy.

Her little daughter Judy, my niece—when nearly five years old, was riding her small bike with her Mummy in Brookwood Cemetery, which was just up the road from their house in Surrey. The cemetery contains military personnel and is quite famous for the resting place of great Generals and other notables. At one side though there is a plot for Nuns and Ecclesiastical folk. The Headstones start with R.I.P. and then Sister . . . usually some Catholic saint's name, you know the sort of thing. Judy, her little face all concerned said 'I feel sorry for that Mrs Rip— poor Mother, losing all her children, look they are all RIP sisters' . . . Sweet isn't it. The lovely things our kids come out with. My own boy who went to St Dunstan's College in Catford, was being driven home by me after school one evening. As we passed through the exit at the end of the curved drive on to the South Circular, there was a hoarding up against the wall of the property opposite. It stated on it in big letters, BILL STICKERS will be prosecuted. Matthew my youngster said 'Who *is* this Bill Stickers?' I burst out laughing as you hear of these howlers but you rarely get personal experience of them, it made my week.

Chapter Thirty Five

I spent many years having more adventures with many other *crazy* happenings. The story is just as colourful and maybe that could be my next book?

I lived an adventuresome life with my cat Willy Wonka until he passed on, I love cats. He was the most interesting *moggie* I ever owned and a great loss. Seal point Siamese cats are super intelligent, he used the loo if he got caught short and 'fetched' when I threw a toy. I sure hope that I will see him again in the afterlife.

I am quite looking forward to seeing what comes next, it is a challenging thought, but I am not afraid. In the past, I used to doubt that there was *anything* once we finish our life span. Since hearing family tales and enduring personal *'oddities'—I* now have to admit that I am keeping a very open mind about death. I think I would be pretty stupid not to, just talk to any geriatric nurse, they will tell you of some amazing happenings on their wards.

So right now, my life consists of observation mainly. I have grown my children, worked, kept things together and done my best. This is what most elderly folk will tell you I guess. I am trying to let go, my job is done now. I have to watch the kids make their own decisions about life and hope that my initial instruction will suffice. They seem to be doing a sterling job despite some dreadful challenges, I am awfully proud of them.

I paint a lot and read hugely. I decided that this story was worthy of putting down for my Grandchildren but I guess they would have to be old enough to read it as some of it is a bit gruesome. I have really enjoyed writing it, even despite some of the memories being difficult and harrowing. I wish I could have chosen nicer men to love.

So, I have finished—some of it is sad, some of it amusing. I hope I haven't recalled any facts that aren't true, I have written only what I have been told by relatives. I should have liked to come up with a great philosophical saying to sound wise and a person of substance, for my final words. I can only repeat that old adage 'What doesn't break you, makes you stronger'.

Finally, don't let life crush you. I have always refused to be made to stay down. Spirit, optimism, energy, hope—these are the watch words. So with these thoughts and the inescapable fact that a new day will dawn and nothing EVIL will last forever, I bid you Good Luck and Goodbye.

THE END

Epilogue

In writing the Epilogue to this account, I would just like to say that my opinions although strongly voiced, are just mine and I don't mean to cause offence with them. It is just that how often does an ordinary person get the chance to air her views? Not too often in the real world . . . unless a politician (and then it's generally the end of their career.) but writing something which one hopes will be read by many, is a God given chance and as age brings wisdom and experience, I believe that I have something worth saying.

About the Author

At the request of Annie Scott's family, her intriguing and gripping life story was written by her. Thanks to an excellent memory, she can recall most of the past 65 years in detail. All who read it said 'Publish.' So in the winter of her life and from her home in Kent she decided to do just that. Alas her family are rather far flung—but with Skype, she is able to keep in close contact with three children and six grandchildren. She lives happily reading, painting and watching films which teach her so much about the world she lives in and would love to see before she becomes too arthritic. Armchair travelling is so nice and there is so much to see and learn about. Having had a meagre post war education, she is glad that books fill the gaps of knowledge that she yearns to obtain.

Lightning Source UK Ltd.
Milton Keynes UK
UKOW02f0339051114

241080UK00002B/12/P